PRAISE FOR *BEYOND SATISFACTION*

"Breanne always provides clear and specific help for customer experiences that exceeds what I could create on my own. She truly is a course design rockstar."
— Chris Guillebeau, NYT Bestselling Author, The $100 Startup

"Breanne's powerful blend of learning strategies and their application to the online marketplace has completely changed my business. If you're ready to build your next highly profitable online course, program or workshop but don't want to settle for less-than-transformational results, you need to read 'Beyond Satisfaction'."
— Tara Gentile, Creator of Quiet Power Strategy®

Beyond Satisfaction

The secret to crafting a profitable online course that will change lives

BREANNE DYCK

Foreword by Jason Van Orden

ISBN-13: 978-1-539186-52-6
ISBN-10: 1-539186-52-0

Please direct inquiries to:
MNIB Consulting Inc.
concierge@mnibconsulting.com
http://mnibconsulting.com

For Grandma
who inspired in me a love of learning
and of good books.

*"He who would learn to fly
one day must learn to stand and
walk and run and climb and dance;
one cannot fly into flying."*
—Friedrich Neitzsche

Table of Contents

Foreword

by Jason Van Orden

In 2005, I sat in my New York City studio checking my email when I got a life-changing message. "You've got money!" stated the subject line of the email from Paypal. I'd received the sum of $197.

This email was far more valuable to me than the amount deposited in my account. It represented a new level of financial freedom. A total stranger had decided my knowledge was valuable enough to him that he'd sent money through the Internet in exchange for a course that I'd created, and that I'd send back to him also through the Internet.

It felt like alchemy. I was exchanging ones and zeroes that I created, as if from thin air, for money. At that moment, I knew that if I could sell my knowledge once, I could do it ten, a hundred or even a thousand times. The Internet had just provided me a way to do something I loved—teach—and get paid really well to do it.

Having since sold several million dollars' worth of digital courses and online learning experiences to thousands of students in dozens of countries around the world, I can certainly attest to the viability of online courses as a business model. If you're reading this, I can assume you offer online courses (or you're thinking about doing so in the near future). I can also safely assume that you want to grow your income and impact by selling more digital courses to more people. If that's the case, then you're reading the right book.

A lot has changed since I created my first online course in 2005. The tools for designing and publishing course materials on the Internet were limited back then, but it didn't stop me or thousands of other enterprising consultants, coaches and thought leaders from translating their knowledge and expertise into Internet-based training.

In some ways, it's only gotten better. There's never been a better time than now to offer online courses and learning experiences. New tools and services make it push-button easy for anyone to produce and publish learning content on the Internet. Course marketplaces like Udemy and Lynda.com have helped to push online learning into the mainstream.

However, as fast as the barrier to entry has lowered, noise in the marketplace has risen, making it increasingly difficult to attract (and keep) the attention of your ideal customers. In addition, less scrupulous marketers offering sub-par products have left customers disillusioned and jaded with online courses. A glut of offers has driven prices downward for businesses who don't know how to compensate for these market forces.

Things continue to change and mature, ultimately for the better. But the truth is that online course creators who don't adapt to the shifting expectations of their target customers will see their profits suffer. It's no longer sufficient to simply satisfy your students if you want to grow your business. To continue growing, you need to delight your customers so they stick around, buy again and motivate others to buy from you as well.

Thankfully, the thoughtful approach that Breanne lays out in this book provides you with the tools you need to not just create profitable courses, but learning experiences that generate transformation for your customers and place you and your business at the forefront of your industry.

I admire many things about Breanne, including her love of spreadsheets and tabletop board games. But more relevant to you is that I admire her ability to turn vital concepts into actionable systems that you can benefit from right away.

And so, dear reader, I can confidently say that by applying what you learn in the pages of this book, "You've got money!"

Introduction to the Second Edition

Over the past several years, my inbox has been increasingly inundated with emails from authors, marketers, podcasters and bloggers all talking about one thing: online courses.

Email after email, from every corner of the on-line world, extolling the virtues of getting into the online teaching game, exclaiming that online courses are the perfect solution for scaling and growing a business.

I am, of course, intensely interested in this trend.

Five years ago, I was working at a technical college, managing the curriculum that would be used by thousands of students each year. Keeping students enrolled through the duration of their two-year program wasn't just a good idea in theory; it was vital to our ability to justify the time, energy and money that were being poured into our school and department as a whole.

As I made the transition to running my own online consulting company, I watched as more and more entrepreneurs began to recognize the opportunities that online courses promised—opportunities to grow their revenue and dramatically increase their impact.

Along the way, I started to observe the same underlying challenges in this world of online entrepreneurship as in the world of traditional higher education: attrition was causing customers—the lifeblood of *any* business—to disappear.

That observation led to the publication of the first edition of *Beyond Satisfaction*, a guide for online business owners who wanted to develop their business with world-class online training products.

In the time since that first edition was published, though, the world of online business has continued to evolve and change.

A few years ago, you could still differentiate yourself by just creating a course. That alone was a unique selling proposition, and it was enough to attract customers—often, a lot of them.

At the time, there were no rules; even quality was relative. In the absence of any benchmarks for what a remarkable learning experience could look like, course creators were left to make up the rules as they went along. And so they did—through trial and error, experimentation and testing, the formulas and step-by-step methods were developed and refined.

Now, many of those same innovators have started teaching their methods, and their students are going on to start their own online training businesses, patterning themselves after their mentors and soaking up as much wisdom from them as they can.

And therein lies the danger.

You see, as this tidal wave of online courses gains speed and volume, it's becoming more and more important to make your own way. To not just follow the formulas or apply someone else's three-step method, but to carve out your own methods for success.

In this revised and expanded edition of *Beyond Satisfaction*, I aim to show you how to do this by focusing on the underlying principles of transformative learning.

With all-new case studies and action steps, this new edition makes it even easier for you to apply the principles to your own courses and programs. New sections—even whole chapters—have been added, on topics such as the importance of customer experience, the completion conundrum, gathering and using feedback and where the online course marketplace is headed next.

Throughout the book I'll also be directing you to a brand-new readers-only area of the *Beyond Satisfaction* website. This area contains a number of resources, guides and worksheets to help you apply the concepts outlined in this book. If you like, you can get a sneak peek at these resources here: *http://beyondsatisfactionbook.com/bonuses*

And, of course, the entire text has been updated to provide greater depth, more examples and increased relevance to today's online business owner.

I can't wait for you to experience all that the new *Beyond Satisfaction* has to offer.

I hope you love it!

—*Breanne Dyck*

Part I

The Customer Experience

1

The Key to Creating
Impactful Courses

There's a killer lurking in your course.

An insidious assassin, creeping through the shadows and making your participants just... disappear.

If you're observant, you'll find the clues: a trail of refund requests and unopened emails that reveal participants who have dropped out. But unless you take action, you'll never be able to uncover the reasons they've failed to complete the program. You'll never even find the bodies.

Your participants—your customers—will just up and vanish.

They won't finish the course; they won't even open the last modules. They'll never respond to follow-ups or give testimonials. And they'll never become the type of ardent fans who buy again and again and again.

The killer is attrition. Its weapons of choice are lack of interest, dissatisfaction and a lack of results. When attrition is left to roam freely amongst your participants, your course fails to have the lasting, transformative impact it should, and your business growth dies along with those vanishing customers.

How do you capture and disarm this deadly foe? The same way you stop a stealth assassin: you put safeguards in place to prevent attack, you follow the clues to root out his identity and finally you hunt down and capture the culprit.

But before we get into that, let me ask you a question:

Why are you creating an online course in the first place?

For many people, the answer that first comes to mind is one of two things.

One, you believe that creating an online course will give you more *time.* By leveraging your work and turning it into a digital product, you can work one-to-many instead of one-on-one. This then allows you to serve the same number of people in dramatically less time.

The second reason I often hear is *money.* "Teach what you know" is held up as a tried-and-tested way to create a sustainable online business. It seems as though every day there's a new rags-to-riches story being published about someone who is now making money hand over fist with their online training programs.

What I've discovered, though, is that those who build truly successful online businesses don't cite money or time as their primary motivators. Instead, they are creating online courses because they are seeking to have a *bigger impact on more lives.*

I'm guessing that you want that, too, and that's why you're reading this book right now.

The Three Rs for Creating Impact in Your Online Training Business

I've worked on some great products, and I've helped to pull some less-than-great ones out of the fire. I've worked on big courses and small workshops. Along the way, I've learned a lot about what really helps participants create change in their lives and achieve their goals.

Here's what I've found: there are three Rs which make the difference between a course that has an impact and one that doesn't.

The first is **retention,** and it's the most foundational of the three. If participants request a refund or drop out early, there's no hope for you to have an impact on them. In this way, retention is the opposite of attrition; when participants are retained, they will actually *use* the training provided.

Once retained, you can then focus on turning those participants into powerful advocates for your business. This is the second R: **referrals**. When a course generates a flood of referrals, the potential reach and impact of that course is multiplied. To do that, of course, it's not enough to simply retain participants; you must also ensure that they are satisfied enough with their experience to tell others.

Satisfaction alone, though, is not enough (thus the title of this book!). Just because someone is *happy* with their progress doesn't mean they've *achieved* their ultimate goal. After all, does helping someone successfully navigate one particular challenge mean that you have done everything you can to impact their life?

No, of course not. You're more than a one-trick pony.

That's why the third R is **repeat buyers**. When you can help someone get from A to B, then later help them get from B to C and then from C to D, you end up having a much more significant impact than if you'd only served them once.

Retention, referrals and repeat buyers: whether you are creating a large-scale DIY program intended to reach thousands or revising a small group coaching program for a handful of people, the three Rs remain the same.

Without them, you can't have the impact you want, you can't build the business you want and you can't live the life you want.

The question that remains, of course, is, *How do you do that?*

That's what the rest of this book will show you. By the time you're finished, you'll not only know how to answer that question, you'll be able to start applying it to your business immediately.

Caution: Watch Out for Magic Bullet Seekers

When you *do* apply the strategies in this book, you'll find yourself consistently getting better retention, amazing referrals and piles of repeat buyers.

But as you continue to develop and scale your business, you'll also encounter a subset of participants that will defy any and all of your attempts to keep them engaged.

I call these people the *magic bullet seekers.* These are the people who bounce from idea to idea, product to product, course to course in search of an easy solution.

They see themselves as having a track record of failures; none of the products they've bought in the past have worked. They come to you looking for an easy fix, and when you can't provide it, they get disillusioned. They're the ones who call you a scam artist or say you've sold out. They get ticked off at you—and then continue on their search for the *next* magic bullet.

Now, you *may* be able to retain some magic bullet seekers and convert them into advocates for your business through the practices described in this guide. But the truth is, most of them won't bite. They'll false start and then blame you, and there's nothing you can do about it.

What's important to realize is that these participants aren't being caught and killed by your course's silent killer. They're just transients, passing through: there one day, gone the next. So don't waste your time trying to solve the problems of magic bullet seekers.

Now, with that in mind, let's get started.

2

The Quest for Bigger Business Growth (and Better Learning Experiences)

Every so often, I'll get on a call with a prospective client that starts something like this:

> **Me:** So, tell me how your course is doing!
>
> **Them:** You know, I get really great feedback, but I just feel like something's missing. Like it could be better somehow.
>
> **Me:** Better? what do you mean by that? What does a *better* course actually look like?

Them: ... *crickets...*

Perhaps you can relate.

We all know that there are advantages to building "better" products, but when's the last time you stopped to think about what that actually means?

What does a successful course look like—to you and your customers?

We'll go into that in depth over the next several chapters, but for now, let's start with one very basic premise: it's your customers who ultimately determine whether your product is successful or not.

They're the ones who buy, thus generating revenue. They're the ones who spread the word about your product, thus garnering you referrals. They're the ones whose lives are changed (or not) by your product.

In every way that matters, really, your customers drive your success.

It All Starts with Customer Experience

It should come as no surprise, then, that research has shown time and time again that one of the most strategic investments you can make to help your business grow is in creating a remarkable customer experience.

There are dozens (if not hundreds) of factors that influence customer experience, including whether you fulfilled your promises, the value received for time spent, an emphasis on problem solving in customer service, treating customers personally and as "real people" and so on.

Yet for as much as we might talk about customer service, we often don't get how big a deal customer experience really is.

Once, I was talking with someone about an online course she'd taken from a Big-Name Internet Personality. I'd just mentioned that I help people grow their online teaching businesses when she leaned over to me and confided, "It was so bad, I'll never buy from him again."

Ouch.

And yet, this is just the tip of the iceberg when it comes to the impact that focusing on creating remarkable customer experiences can have on your business. Below are just a few examples of how a positive customer experience can affect your business.

Remarkable Customer Experiences Help You Sell More

According to a 2012 report by the Temkin Group, companies who are all-stars in the customer experience game enjoy roughly 19% higher "likely to recommend" scores, compared to the industry average.

(Note: links to references cited and other resources are included in the online resources page at ***http://beyondsatisfactionbook.com/bonuses*)*

If percentages aren't your thing, here's what that means: when you provide a great customer experience, an additional one out of every five customers will give you a referral.

Oh, and don't forget this is a multiplicative effect, which means that it grows exponentially over time. If you have 125 customers, improving your customer experience could lead to 25 more referrals. And *those* 25 new customers will likely *also* add five *more* referrals. And *those* five will also add *one more* referral.

All of a sudden, you've now got 156 customers from your original 125—without having to change your sales process, launch again or grow your list.

Better Experiences Mean You Can Charge More

In 2002, an international team of researchers explored the relationship between price and satisfaction when it came to buying a new car. They found that if customers felt as though a dealer's prices were fair—regardless of whether the prices were objectively high or low—they were likely to be satisfied with their purchase.

This makes sense; no one feels satisfied if they think they have been ripped off!

But price relates to customer experience in other, more subtle ways. For example, researchers from Stanford and CalTech wanted to see if price affected the perceived quality of a bottle of wine. They found that the answer is yes: price perception is a huge factor in determining whether a customer feels you've provided a quality product or service. If you want to justify higher prices, customers will expect more before they'll be satisfied.

The good news is that once you've satisfied a customer, they also show more price tolerance. In other words, if you can blow someone's socks off, they will be more willing to pay premium prices later.

Great Customer Experiences Get People To Buy More

Finally, research has also shown that you can dramatically ramp up how often people buy (and how long they continue to buy from you) by improving your customer experience.

The *Harvard Business Review*, for example, looked at two global $1B+ businesses to see how customer experience mapped to revenues. The findings were dramatic: in just one year, customers who had the best experiences spent *140% more* than those who had the poorest experiences. That's *after* adjusting for how often the customer would need the type of product/service sold; this is pure revenue gain, strictly attributed to the quality of the customer experience.

But beyond that, when they looked at ongoing purchases—specifically, subscription- and membership-based revenues—they found that you could predict how long someone would *continue* to buy from the company by looking at their customer experience.

With a poor experience, a customer only had a 43% chance of staying a member the next year;

the average customer in this category would cancel their membership in just over a year.

Compare those figures to a member who had a great experience; they would have a 74% chance of still being a paid subscriber the next year. On average, they would stick around for *six years*.

That adds up to a lot of revenue.

So Now What?

Intuitively, we all know that bad customer experiences cost our businesses money and good ones help us grow. And now you've seen the research that shows just how dramatic the impact can be.

But here's the thing: **despite knowing this, many business owners still aren't willing to invest the time or resources to create products that provide a truly world-class customer experience.**

Here's what's also true: you can't afford to be one of those business owners.

So the next logical question is, *How do you create a remarkable learning experience?*

To answer that, we need to examine the three types of participants that will end up in your course.

Tara Gentile's Remarkable Customer Experience (Case Study)

One business owner who spends a *lot* of time focused on transforming her customer experience is Tara Gentile.

For the past several years, Tara has been refining her methods for helping entrepreneurs break through their earning plateaus and design businesses that are prepared to scale. She started by offering one-on-one coaching before turning her expertise into a multiple-six-figure online program.

People loved it.

The results were great, referrals were strong and Tara ended up with many customers who were fans for life. And yet, as she offered the program over and over, she discovered that there were a few challenges that kept popping up that she just couldn't seem to solve.

One of the main problems was with completion rates. Simply put, while those who *did* complete the program got amazing results, too many participants would get bogged down in the early modules and never move past them.

This was compounded by the fact that, as in many programs, there was a fair amount of foundational work required before participants could get to what *they* felt was the good stuff. When they would look back on their experience as a whole, they could see how all the pieces fit together—but when they were in the thick of it, they struggled.

Finally, as time went on, Tara (and I) started noticing that the program wasn't selling as easily as it had in the past. Prospective customers were no longer new to online courses, and they had started to become jaded. They started to doubt whether they could—or should—commit several months of their lives to taking another course, when they had purchased and failed to complete so many others already.

It was when we realized this last challenge that the lightbulb moment occurred.

The solution wasn't to try to "fix" her course by removing modules, breaking content up differently or hiring coaches to work with the clients.

The solution was to create an entirely different end-to-end experience.

We started by examining her market. While her ideal customers were hesitating to invest in expensive courses or coaching programs, they *were* still spending time and money on training. They would, for example, spend a full week watching her on CreativeLive or take days away from their business to attend a conference or retreat.

Then, we looked for ways to make her program look and feel more like those experiences. The solution: what had been offered as a two-, three- and four-month program would now be compressed into a two-day virtual retreat.

As she considered the implications of this, Tara realized that this all-new experience had the potential to solve the other problems, as well. No longer would people get bogged down in second-guessing themselves; the shorter timespan would force them to trust their instincts and keep moving forward. And by asking people to take two days away from their business, the risk that they would drop off midway through would be greatly diminished.

What Tara didn't expect, though, was just how successful the new experience would be.

For one, the completion rate was a perfect 100%. Every single person who started out during the first session was still there, active and participating, at the end of the second day—even the Australians, for whom the program ran through the night.

It wasn't just about the improved completion rate, though. The speed with which participants started reporting results was incredible. In a matter of days, not weeks or months, people were sharing the actions they had taken and the changes they had made as a result of the program. The quick-start effect of the shorter program meant that participants were better able to keep moving forward and see how everything fit together in the process.

Finally, Tara found that the new experience she had designed made it easier to sell, too. Her most recent launch sold out completely before the cart had closed; she didn't even have time to send a "last chance" email.

Buoyed by this success, Tara is now redeveloping her entire product suite to focus on offering more experiences like these. She's discovered the key to creating an experience that her customers really get excited about—and benefit from.

Three Types of Participants

When Massive Open Online Courses (MOOCs) were first introduced in 2008, they took the world of higher education by storm. Media platforms heralded MOOCs as the vanguard of a new era in education: online learning, taught by some of the world's best instructors, available to thousands of students from around the globe for *free*.

Education, they claimed, was an industry ripe for disruption. Technology and Internet accessibility had finally made it possible to provide interactive eLearning on a scale never seen before. Big-name institutions like MIT and Harvard jumped on the bandwagon, launching platform EdX into the limelight with great fanfare.

It didn't take long, though, before the headlines started to change.

By 2013, the *New York Times* website featured such headlines as "The Trouble With Online College," "Universities Rethinking Their Use of Massive Online Courses" and "After Setbacks, Online Courses Are Rethought." In each article, the message was the same: almost no one that registers for a MOOC ever does anything with it. A study from the University of Pennsylvania found that of the millions of students enrolling in these courses, only half viewed even a single lecture. Less than 5% would ever complete the course.

This kicked off a flurry of research and investigation in the educational community. What was the problem? Why weren't students completing these courses? What researchers discovered is that while there are many factors that affect students' likelihood of completing a course, there are three basic types of students that you'll find enrolling in online courses:

- Active Participants,

- Passive Participants and

- Lurkers.

Each type comes to a course with different goals, desires and needs. And each has a different likelihood of dropping out.

This is incredibly relevant; working with clients over the past several years, I've learned that these three types of students aren't just found in the world of higher education and MOOCs. Independent online business owners also encounter them as participants in their online courses and programs.

The good news is that when you understand how each of these types approaches your course, you can better target your marketing and teaching to suit them. By doing that, you not only keep them more engaged, you also make them more likely to stick around and be successful.

So let's take a closer look at each of the three types.

The Holy Grail: Active Participants

Estimates peg the number of Active Participants in any given online course at about 5–10% of total enrollments. These are the people that read everything, watch every video, listen to every audio (twice!), do every exercise/quiz/activity, start and comment on discussions and generally go out of their way to ensure that they are squeezing every possible ounce from their learning experience.

It should come as no surprise, then, that these Active Participants are also the ones who are most likely to complete the course *and* the ones most likely to see lasting results. Your Active Participants are the ones who give you rock-star testimonials that even *you* can't believe are true, the ones that make you think, *They got all that as a result of my course!?*

The Seemingly Uninterested: Lurkers

You know the ones. Lurkers are the people who log into the course website to check it out, maybe skim through the first module, but generally don't do much beyond that. They have whole sections of their hard drive dedicated to eBooks they've never read. Their inbox is full of unopened email courses.

Lurkers make up an estimated 10–15% of your course participants. And if you're not careful, they're the ones who will drive you *absolutely nuts*. I mean, you're probably glad they decided to buy (more money is always good), but it can actually be quite uncomfortable.

It's easy to feel like they're not actually learning anything or gaining any value from the experience, that you've somehow ripped them off. Top consultant and bestselling author Alan Weiss calls this *scope seep:* the feeling that somehow you've failed to provide enough value and must somehow do *more* to compensate.

The temptation is to try to adjust your curriculum to cater to Lurkers, but as we'll discuss in just a moment, this approach can end up doing more harm than good.

The Vast Majority: Passive Participants

And then there's the rest: 70–80% of students in online courses are Passive Participants. They read the materials, watch the videos, maybe even take some notes now and again. They have particular goals in mind and are willing to put in the effort so long as they can see how the task at hand gets them closer to where they want to be.

Otherwise, they are there primarily to consume information; they're unlikely to participate in discussions, complete activities or worksheets or do any type of assessments (such as self-tests, surveys or actual quizzes) unless they have to in order to progress.

If you were to assign grades, these would be your solid C students. They won't rock your world, but they're definitely learning and progressing. They're simply more likely to pick and choose the bits that feel important to them, focus on that and then ignore or discard the rest.

Different Types of Participants Want Different Things...

Clearly, we all love rock-star testimonials and want to see each and every one of our students experiencing massive results. As such, the temptation is to try to create a course that will convince Lurkers and Passive Participants to start acting more like Active Participants.

But this never works.

See, when it comes right down to it, no two prospective customers want exactly the same thing from your course. Some will come to you seeking quick results. They want something they can pick up, skim through and put down. Rinse, repeat.

When prospects come to your program with this expectation, they are naturally going to behave more like Lurkers. For these customers, a win looks like grabbing a quick reference—checklists, templates or scripts—so they can get quick wins without actually investing a whole bunch of time mastering the details.

Other prospects come to you with the goal of solving a very specific problem. They'll read your sales page and hone in on the *one specific bullet point* that speaks to that problem. Even if they *aren't* struggling with the other things your course addresses, the promise of solving that one problem is tantalizing enough to get them to enroll.

When they finally get into the program, these customers exhibit behavior characteristic of Passive Participants: they'll pick and choose what to work on, focusing in on those areas that they can clearly relate back to that very specific goal.

Of course, a small handful of customers come to our program because they really do want it all and are willing to do what it takes to get it. They are hungry to not just learn at a conceptual level; they are committed to getting their hands dirty. Worksheets, case studies, coaching calls, discussion boards, practice material, quizzes, homework ... the more the better. Bring it on.

If you can provide them with the framework and tools they seek, these customers will become your most Active Participants—and your most successful ones, too.

... But They Often Don't Know What They Want

Calculating how many participants in your courses fall into each of these three groups is a useful exercise on its own. If nothing else, the rough percentages provide a benchmark for knowing whether your overall completion rates are in the ballpark.

But there's more to it than that.

Recently, I participated in a fascinating discussion on Facebook with some top online marketers about refund rates. While many boasted of a sub-1% refund rate, others admitted that their rate was much higher—up to 20% in some cases. This is not unusual for the industry, though you'll rarely see someone openly admit that their refund rate is that high.

There are a number of factors that can cause someone to request a refund, but in the end, they all boil down to one thing: unmet expectations. Whether the customer expected to feel better about their purchase, they expected the material to be delivered differently or they expected to see different results, the result is the same: a disgruntled customer that wants their money back.

The problem arises because most customers come to our programs *believing* and *intending* themselves to be Active Participants. When they fail to meet that expectation, they have two choices: to blame themselves, or to blame us.

When they blame *us*, they'll usually request a refund.

When they blame *themselves*, they may request a refund—or they may get down on themselves, believing they are the reason for their failure.

Both outcomes are bad for business, but the latter is especially insidious because customers who blame themselves will be less likely to trust themselves to follow through in the future. It's why we're now seeing so many customers making blanket refusals to buy "yet another course"—they don't trust themselves to do the work to make it worthwhile.

The Solution: Focus On Your Perfect Participant

In an ideal world, we would only attract the right participants into our courses.

Their goals would perfectly align with the content of our courses, and so they would do every exercise, read every resource, watch every video and see massive results. We'd only ever have Active Participants, and everything would be right with the world: our retention rate would be 100%, our referrals would skyrocket and all our customers would hungrily await our next product.

In practice, this doesn't happen.

The simple truth is this: you will never eliminate Lurkers and Passive Participants from your courses.

And while great curriculum *can* help encourage increased participation—and we'll talk a lot more about ways to do that in the coming chapters—you (and your business) will be better served by focusing your attention on those who actually want to learn and succeed, rather than those who are just seeking quick fixes or partial transformations.

Ultimately, getting the right people into your course is vital to your success.

If you attract the wrong types of people into your course, you'll never solve your retention problems. You'll also never get the rave reviews, repeat buyers and referrals that you're looking for.

This is especially challenging when our *customers* don't know exactly what they need. We're lucky, in fact, if they know what they *want.*

The role of helping customers self-select in (or out) of your program, then, falls to you.

That requires you to know exactly *who* you want most in your course: the person I call your Perfect Participant. We'll dig into the Perfect Participant in the Your Turn section that follows, but before we get to that, here's a case study that shows exactly *how* and *why* it's so important.

How Marie Poulin Found Her Perfect Participants (Case Study)

Marie Poulin was at a crossroads.

Her boutique web design business was thriving and in demand, and her client list read like a who's who of online business: Marie Forleo, Natalie MacNeil, Alive in Berlin and others.

While this allowed her to command premium rates, it also had a trade-off: Marie was regularly turning away new clients that she might have otherwise loved to help and *still* her calendar was overflowing.

Her business model needed to change, or she was going to burn out.

Marie knew she wanted to create some kind of digital product: a course, an eBook, something that would allow her to expand her reach (and grow her business) without having to invest a huge amount of time. Her initial idea was to take what she was doing as a web designer and teach it to clients who couldn't afford her.

But then I asked her the question that changed everything: Are these things that people are actually asking you for?

The answer was no. She wished people would ask her these questions, but no one was really pounding down her door to get answers.

It was time to go back to the drawing board and find her Perfect Participant. To do that, I encouraged Marie to think about what questions she *was* answering on a daily and weekly basis. The answer, she realized, was right in front of her: her peers were always asking questions about how she'd managed to make the leap from freelance web designer to in-demand digital strategist.

They were her perfect participants.

Within an hour of having this realization, Marie sent me this email:

Marie Poulin
10 mins · Vancouver · Edited

Looking for some honest feedback... putting myself out there.
So I am in the midst of creating my first online course, which is based on
the strategy process that I go through with my clients.
Initially I was thinking this would be a sort of "digital strategy for everyday
people" kinda thing, targeted at small business owners... but the more I
think about it, the more I wonder if I shouldn't be targeting other
designers/peers.
Basically, using digital strategy to level up your design business, so you
can start charging much higher rates on your projects, and actually
offering more value. There is only so much you can get away with
charging for design, generally speaking... but the reason I've been able to
move from $4,000 websites to $15,000 websites? STRATEGY + Insight.
is this something any of you would actually be interested in -- learning how
to move from designer to digital strategist? Moving from small potatoes
freelance to small business owner?
I would see this as part resource, part how-to, and part "sneak peek" at
how I run my business. If this is something you'd be interested in, please
let me know. If you think it's silly, you can tell me that too 😊
Thanks guys! ♡

Like · Comment

✓ Seen by 6

 YES, I would ABSOLUTELY be interested in this. I'm
actively moving toward digital strategist but I know I have SO MUCH to learn -
and I'm definitely NOT charging $15k/site, which would be awesome. If you
build it, I will come. 😊
5 mins · Unlike · 👍 1

 Yes yes yes please.
2 mins · Like

 YES
2 secs · Like

Write a comment...

From there, Marie wasted no time; she
quickly put together the high-level details of
what she was thinking and started making
invitations to a private pilot.

Before long, Marie had more than a
dozen eager testers chomping at the bit and
$5,000 in her pocket. Her Perfect Partici-

pants had clearly identified themselves to her. But before she could provide them with massive value, she still needed to know more about who they were and what they needed.

Marie quickly invited all her testers into a private Facebook group and encouraged them all to share their struggles so she could dive right in and start assembling tools, exercises and resources to support them. Within days, participants were already messaging her, saying, "Holy crap, the course hasn't even started yet and I'm already getting so much value."

From there on out, Marie shared the material as she developed it, agilely responding to participants' exact needs. And they loved her for it.

When it finally came time to launch the course publicly, Marie sold out the program. She didn't have a big list or the backing of big-name influencers. Instead, she focused on providing exactly what her Perfect Participants needed, and she reaped the rewards.

Digital Strategy School went on to earn more than six figures in revenue its first year, and Marie's business model is now almost entirely product-based.

Your Turn!

Discover Your Perfect Participant

Your Turn! sections appear throughout this book as a way for you to put into practice what you have just read. Each is accompanied by an additional resource, download or guide, which you can find at http://beyondsatisfactionbook.com/bonuses.

Let's get one thing clear, right off the bat. Discovering your Perfect Participant is *not* the same as doing yet another customer avatar or ideal client profile exercise.

For one, those exercises always have you generalizing characteristics about your customers across the lifetime of their engagement with your business. But as we all know, the purpose of creating a course or a program is to *create a change* in the customer. Say you have two courses: one that serves more as an introduction, and one that goes deeper.

Are the ideal customers for these two courses the same?

Of course not!

That's why when you set out to discover your Perfect Participant, rather than generalizing you need to focus extremely specifically on the person who would:

- Read your sales page and get so excited that it's exactly what they need right now that they'd...

- Go straight for the buy button without a second thought and then...

- Be an all-star throughout the program

Ideally, in fact, this Perfect Participant should be someone you *actually know.* A one-on-one client, a participant in a past offering, someone you've mentored—whenever you are thinking about your Perfect Participant, it's always best to have a real person in mind.

Who They Are at That Moment in Time

Your Perfect Participant isn't just a real person, though. They also happen to exist at a particular moment in time. As such, they come to your program already having a specific set of experiences, knowledge, skills and attitudes.

When you consider your Perfect Participant's starting point, you're able to more easily ensure that your course begins at the right level of complexity. Think of it like establishing prerequisites for a college course. By assuming that your Perfect Participant will have a certain baseline level of knowledge and experience, you can ensure that the training you provide to them will hit the Goldilocks spot: not too easy, not too hard, juuuuuuust right.

Here are some questions to consider to help you clarify this starting point:

1. What do they *already know* about the topic of your course?

2. What *relevant skills* do they already possess?

3. Is there anything they *know about* but aren't *skilled at*?

You can download these questions and several more in a fillable worksheet available at *http://beyondsatisfactionbook.com/bonuses* called the Perfect Participant Guide. This resource will walk you through the entire process.

Identify Their Ideal Outcomes

Of course, your Perfect Participant isn't just defined by who they are *before* they take your program, but also by what *expectations* they bring to the table. After all, before you can meet or exceed your customers' expectations, you have to know what they are.

For that reason, it's worth also considering what experiences, knowledge and skills your Perfect Participant will need to *gain* through the program before they (and you) will deem it a success. Consider things like:

- What they will be doing after completing your course that they didn't know they could or should be doing

- What they will be doing after completing your course that they knew they should be doing, but didn't know how to do beforehand

Not Every Participant Will Be Perfect

Once you have clarity around who, exactly, your Perfect Participant is, you can focus all your energy and attention on serving that person and their needs to the best of your ability.

Of course, not everyone will want or need what your Perfect Participant wants and needs. By focusing on those who *are* perfect, though, you maximize the chances that they will become Active Participants.

Plus, even those customers who aren't a 100% match with your Perfect Participant will be better served because they will be able to more easily self-identify what areas of your program will help them reach their needs. They're more likely to end up as Passive Participants, but even at that, they can still receive remarkable value from your course.

Why?

Because even though retention is a key ingredient for maximizing your impact, it's not the whole story...

Part II

Creating Transformation

4

The Completion
Conundrum

Have you ever heard comments like these?

- "I've bought courses in the past and never used them."

- "I need to focus on implementing what I've already learned."

- "I'm on a course-buying moratorium.'"

I'll bet you have.

Person after person, business after business, course after course, these responses are quickly becoming one of the top reasons that prospective customers aren't buying.

And who can blame them?

In a recent conversation I had with top industry leaders in the online business space, the consensus was that typical refund rates (yes, *refund* rates) are as high as 15–20%, and only 3–4% of those who remain in the program actually complete it.

Three to four percent!

Thus, increasing completion rates has become a red-hot topic amongst online entrepreneurs. Completion is, after all, another way of looking at and talking about retention.

What Is Completion Anyway?

The problem, of course, is that defining what constitutes completion is not exactly an easy task. Is it enough for participants to have...

- Watched every video?

- Downloaded every worksheet?

- Accessed every module?

- Clicked on every email?

Or does completion mean something *more?* Do they need to have *completed* every worksheet, *fin-*

ished every action step and *applied* everything they've learned?

Especially in an online business where you aren't interacting with your participants one-to-one, it can be really hard to know when someone has actually done all the work. In leveraging our time, we're no longer deeply engaged with each client, and when we start to have dozens, hundreds or thousands of students, it's no longer practical to try to keep track of every one.

As a result, the trend is to pay attention to metrics that are relatively easy to measure.

Maybe your video platform will tell you how many people watched your video all the way through, so you use video views as a completion metric. Or your email platform reports how many people clicked through on your emails, so you use that. Or your learning management system allows you to lock content down until a participant clicks a button to unlock the next lesson.

These metrics may be easy to gather, but they all have one major problem: they all assume that consumption of content is an accurate way to measure how much students have learned.

Even on the surface, this is obviously a faulty assumption.

After all, you can't tell me you haven't put a YouTube video on in the background and then continued surfing and reading. Technically, the video played all the way through, so it "completed," but you probably didn't truly hear a word of it.

But the problem goes deeper than that, and it relates directly to our over-reliance on content as a teaching tool.

How Important Is Content for Learning?

Medical students consistently rank neurology as the most difficult medical discipline. The brain is a complex and interwoven piece of anatomy, and the state of neuroscience is constantly changing and evolving. Even students who are strong in all other areas of medicine usually find the brain a tough subject to master.

So a group of researchers from Stanford decided to band together to see if there wasn't a creative way they could simplify this challenging topic. Through the magic of technology (and some old-fashioned ingenuity), they created BrainExplorer, an interactive tabletop interface that simulates how the brain responds to visual stimuli.

Then, they divided a bunch of students, all new to neuroscience, into two groups. One group of students was invited to do free-form experimentation with the tabletop, with no real instruction other than to see what they could figure out about the brain's processing of visual images. The other group of students was presented with a more traditional teaching tool: a neuroscience textbook that described the process.

The results were definitive: **the students who practiced hands-on learning with the interactive model were much more successful than those who had experienced traditional textbook learning.**

(And, just in case you're about to jump on textbooks as the problem—the same experiment was conducted with students learning through video rather than reading textbooks. Same results.)

After the post-test, the researchers switched the groups around. The students that started with the textbook went to the tabletop; the ones that started on the tabletop went and used the textbook.

Then the students were given one final assessment, and the findings were clear. While both groups of students showed improvements in their final post-test, those who experienced hands-on learning before experiencing traditional text or video learning got far superior results.

By the way, did you know that researchers have identified seven things you can do in your videos to make students more likely to take action after watching? Find out what they are at http:// beyondsatisfactionbook.com/bonuses.

Content Consumption Does Not Lead to Maximum Impact

The implications of this Stanford study are clear: if you want to maximize the impact of your work on your participants' lives, it's not enough for them to consume all your content.

In fact, it's possible for a participant to have a *low* completion rate and *still* achieve a major transformation as a result of your program.

After all, haven't you had the experience where someone gets into just the first module of your program and they are *blown away* by some key light-bulb moment that changes *everything* for them?

Even if you haven't had that experience personally, I'm sure you know someone who has.

And here's the thing: if a customer believes that they have received significant value from you, even if that value comes from just part of your course, then that means your work has had an impact.

As such, it's entirely possible to have a successful program that has a significant impact *and* has relatively low completion rates.

Value Is in the Eye of the Beholder

Don't get me wrong. I don't want you to throw completion rates out entirely, or imagine that retention doesn't matter. It does.

After all, even if your participants can experience a transformation from just part of your course, won't they experience a much bigger transformation if they do it *all?* Of course the answer is yes; results and impact are multiplied when your participants work through everything you have to offer them.

But the simple truth is that it is our customers, not us, who decide whether our work has been valuable to them. Value *is* in the eye of the beholder, and a dissatisfied customer is extremely harmful to the long-term health of your business.

Fortunately, as we'll discover in the next chapter, there are a few simple things that can predict whether your customers will be satisfied … or not.

5

Predicting Satisfaction

I remember the first time I was confronted with the reality that higher education is about business first and learning second. I was still working at the technical college, and I was attending a lecture given by a noted guest speaker. The topic? The number one issue facing post-secondary institutions today: student retention.

Why is student retention such a big issue for these schools, you may ask? It's not simply out of an altruistic desire to see students stay in their programs through to graduation so that they get their degree and become successful, contributing members of society.

No, it's because every student who drops out early is a lost customer, which means lost revenue.

Colleges and universities today are in a desperate competition with each other, and not just on the court, in the ice rink or on the turf. As costs have climbed and funding options stagnated, administrators have been forced to become increasingly cost- and revenue-focused.

That's why schools are spending millions of dollars on recruitment and retention, competing with each other to gain new students, keep the ones they've attracted and steal away transfer students. They're not just competing for the best and the brightest. They're competing for bodies to fill seats and pay tuition. And then, they have to keep them there.

This reality has forced educators to face an inconvenient truth: they don't just have students, they have customers. And as anyone who runs a business knows, customers need to be satisfied.

The Vital Importance of Customer Satisfaction

When it comes right down to it, satisfied customers are the driving force behind ongoing revenues—

they're the ones who are most likely to make referrals, give solid reviews and become repeat buyers.

In *Marketing Metrics: The Definitive Guide to Measuring Marketing Performance*, the authors drive this point home, saying: "Customer satisfaction provides a leading indicator of consumer purchase intentions and loyalty."

Put another way: happy customers buy more, more often, and get others to do the same.

When it comes to education, the same is true. According to Ruffalo Noel Levitz (a consultancy that specializes in maximizing post-secondary enrollment), a comprehensive study of more than 27,000 students revealed that "student satisfaction is indeed connected to student persistence, as well as to the word-of-mouth reputation of an institution."

Satisfied students, in other words, are not only less likely to fall victim to attrition. They're also more likely to give positive referrals and reviews, which all build the bottom line.

What Makes a Student Satisfied?

Traditional measures of student satisfaction have largely been centered on the campus experience.

Most surveys ask questions about amenities like the gym, the food service and classroom environments. However, in recent years, researchers have also begun turning their attention to what drives satisfaction in an online learning experience.

What they've found is that there are three main predictors of student satisfaction in online courses:

- The students' engagement with the curriculum materials, known as learner-content interactions,

- The students' interactions with their instructors and

- The students' comfort using the Internet, known as Internet self-efficacy.

The third predictor makes sense; someone who is less comfortable using the Internet will struggle more and be less satisfied in an online learning environment. In fact, I frequently dissuade clients who are trying to reach less-savvy audiences from creating online courses. The overall lower satisfaction—not to mention the increased customer support costs—makes it a challenge rarely worth taking on.

The implications of the other two predictors, though, are less clear. So let's take a deeper dive into how these factors contribute to customer satisfaction—and how to address these predictors in your courses.

The Value of Engaging and Interactive Content

According to the research, the most significant and strongest predictor of student satisfaction is the course content itself. If you want happy students, you need to have well-designed curriculum that encourages students to engage with it.

There are many different tactics and approaches to doing this, but one of the most effective is actually the simplest, as discovered by a team of researchers who wanted to find a way to keep college students enrolled in an introductory psychology course that had a notoriously high attrition rate.

The experiment was deceptively simple: Immediately after the midterm exam, students completed one of two different essay assignments. One group of students were to write a summary of what they had learned about a given topic. The other group was assigned to describe how what they had learned related to their life.

The researchers found that, for those who had done well on their midterms, the assignment made relatively little difference. Those students remained interested in psychology, regardless of which essay they had been asked to write. For them, positive results (and high confidence) resulted in sustained high interest and increased performance over time—not surprising.

But for those who had not done well on the midterms, the results of this study were far more revealing: Those students who had been asked to relate their learning back to their own lives maintained high levels of interest in the course, despite their poor test scores. Those who had been asked to summarize what they learned? Their interest tanked, and their performance suffered as well.

The implications of this study are so important, I feel it's necessary to underscore them:

You can increase retention and student success in your course simply by getting your participants to reflect on what they're doing and how it relates to their life.

Instead of creating theoretical examples or assigning fill-in-the-blank worksheets that are essentially fact checks on the course content, get your students to actually apply what you are teaching them to their own lives and their own situation.

For example, let's say your course is designed to help people eat more healthily. You *could* spend a lot of time explaining what the various macronutrients are, how they affect the body, the impact of one's metabolism and so on and so forth.

Or, you could do what one of my clients, Ali Shapiro, creator of Truce with Food, did: ask your course participants to experiment with eating various things, and then record how those foods made them feel, in order to determine what is healthy for their body.

Even though she knows how nutrition works from a medical perspective, Ali realized that inundating clients with scientific jargon and overloading them with facts wouldn't do much good. On the flip side, the simple act of encouraging participants to note what they were eating and how their bodies reacted helped them immediately apply what they had learned to their everyday lives—so they could truly *know* what was healthy, not just read about it.

This is the magic of relevance and reflection: the more you can tie your course back to participants' lives, the more interested they will be in it. Remind them why they're there, and you'll not only see improved interest levels but also stronger performance, especially among those who doubt their own abilities.

You Are Vital to Student Satisfaction

Of course, it's not just enough to have great content. If that were so, textbooks, blogs and eBooks would have replaced the need for facilitated courses entirely.

It's not surprising, then, that the second strongest predictor of student satisfaction in online learning is their relationship—or potential relationship—with their instructor or other experts.

This is reinforced by the research of Marcia Dixson, who wanted to figure out what it took to really engage students in online courses. Dixson theorized that by incorporating certain types of activities into a course, she would get more engagement. She just wasn't sure what types would be best. Quizzes? Discussion forums? Group projects? Live chat sessions? Email? Hands-on practice and application?

Through extensive study, Dixson found that she was actually trying to answer the wrong question.

Her results indicated that the *type* of activity was irrelevant. There was virtually no difference in student engagement across the different activities.

Instead, the pattern that *did* emerge was that engagement correlated more with interpersonal engagement. When students had multiple ways to interact with each other and with their instructor(s), regardless of what those ways were, they were more highly engaged.

Here's how Dixson summarized her findings: "The path to student engagement, based on this data, is not about the type of activity/assignment but about multiple ways of creating meaningful communication between students and with their instructor—it's all about connections."

It's important to note that these connections can take many forms; as Dixson herself was quick to point out, there is no *one way* to create those connections. Coaching calls, online communities, emails that go to customer support—all of these methods can give your participants confidence that they are not alone on their journey.

And if you aren't willing or able to engage with participants yourself? Consider empowering team members, community managers or even alumni to take on leadership roles and fill in that gap for you, just like teaching assistants do for professors in colleges worldwide.

Finding Nuance in Satisfaction

So, customer satisfaction matters. That much is clear.

It's not just a good idea for its own sake; it's actually one of the biggest drivers of customer retention and business growth.

Of course, we've been talking about satisfaction as though it were one, universal thing, which is a gross oversimplification. There's a great quote in a *Harvard Business Review* article entitled "Why Satisfied Customers Defect":

> According to conventional wisdom, the link between satisfaction and loyalty in markets where customers have choices is a simple, linear relationship: As satisfaction goes up, so does loyalty. But we discovered that the relationship was neither linear nor simple. To a much greater extent than most managers think, completely satisfied cus-

tomers are more loyal than merely satisfied customers.

As we consider satisfaction, then, it's not just a
black-and-white measure. In fact, we'd be far better
off to think of satisfaction as a matter of degrees:
dissatisfied, partially satisfied, mostly satisfied, completely satisfied.

Rather than thinking of the final arbiter of satisfaction as whether customers say yes on a satisfaction survey, then, we need to take a deeper, more
nuanced approach.

6

Beyond Satisfaction

It's easy to look at customer satisfaction as the ultimate measure of our course's success. After all, if customers are happy, who are we to argue?

But as we saw in the previous chapter, satisfaction isn't an all-or-nothing proposition. There are *degrees* of satisfaction, and just because a customer says "yes, I'm satisfied" doesn't mean that you've done everything you can for them.

Not to mention that if you're not careful, satisfaction can become a shiny object in your business. You can get so focused on giving people what they *say* they want that you may be missing out on opportunities to also give them what they really need.

The tendency to focus on satisfaction—almost to the exclusion of everything else—is something I call the Satisfaction Trap.

Why a trap?

Because when you are too focused on what people are saying about your courses, you're missing the more important metric of success: what they are actually *doing* with what they've learned.

After all, as shown in the Stanford neuroscience study cited in Chapter 4, it's taking action that creates the biggest transformation and the most learning for our participants.

Simply put, knowledge without application doesn't create impact.

Here's another way to think about it: my friend Vanessa Van Edwards of Science of People says that reviews or testimonials saying, "That course was so interesting!" are actually the kiss of death.

If the best thing someone can say about a course is that it's interesting, you've failed to do what really matters: help your customers get *results*.

Your Customers Aren't the Real Experts

Most educators chafe at the notion of treating satisfaction as a core success measure for a course or learning experience for one simple reason:

Satisfaction doesn't measure transformation.

After all, customers purchase your course specifically because they *aren't* as expert as you are.

As such, they don't really know what success looks like. They have an *idea*. They can *imagine* what they think their life will be like when they have mastered what you have to offer.

But their lack of competence in the subject area, by definition, means that they can't truly judge their own progress. Have they learned everything they should have? Have they made mistakes? Have they exceeded expectations?

Our participants can't answer those questions on their own, and the competence matrix (pictured below) explains why.

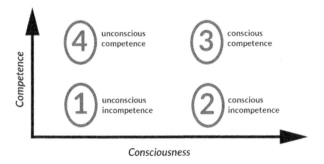

According to Gordon Training International employee Noel Burch, there are four stages of competence that comprise a learning process. For the purposes of the current discussion, stages two and three are the most relevant, but it's worthwhile to briefly discuss all four to provide context.

Stage One: Unconscious Incompetence

The first stage is when one is unconscious of just how incompetent they really are. In other words, this is when they simply don't know what they don't know.

People in this stage may not even recognize there is anything *to* know. Even if they *do* recognize that there's something they lack—some knowledge, some skill, etc.—they don't see how gaining facility in that area will help them.

You'll never find any participants in your course who are at the level of unconscious incompetence. Why? Because if they aren't aware there's something for them to learn, they'll have no reason to buy in the first place!

Stage Two: Conscious Incompetence

At some point, it's like a lightbulb goes on: whether through internal realization or someone pointing it out to them, a person will recognize that they are lacking a skill and that having the skill would make a difference for them. This realization marks their transition to the second stage.

Consciously incompetent customers know they have a problem, and they're painfully aware of how it's affecting them. They are actively looking for solutions, which makes this the perfect opportunity to start making some sales. That's why, for the most part, when a participant first enrolls in your course they will be at this stage of their learning journey.

They are, however, still incompetent. They don't actually have the skills. They just now know exactly how much they lack.

Stage Three: Conscious Competence

Now, you can't just leave someone in conscious incompetence and expect that to be enough; after all, no one *likes* feeling incompetent.

That's why the biggest thing you can do for customers is to help them move from stage two, conscious incompetence, to stage three, conscious competence.

At the level of conscious competence, your participants finally feel as though they know how to do something. It will still take them more effort—it won't feel natural yet—but they'll be gaining confidence and starting to feel like they're getting it.

Remember, though, when they are at this stage, your participants are not yet full experts. They'll still make mistakes, and they'll still need your guidance and support as they continue their learning journey.

Stage Four: Unconscious Competence

Finally, the highest stage of learning in the competence model is when you have achieved unconscious competence.

This is the point where you are *so good at what you do that you don't even realize it.*

A great example of unconscious competence is the everyday skill of walking. Most of us really have no idea what all happens that allows us to walk. If we were to try to teach it to someone else, we'd struggle to give anything more than a high-level overview: Lift one leg. Swing it forward. Put it down. Shift your weight onto that leg. Now lift up the other leg. Swing it forward. And so on.

But of course, this belies the true complexity of walking. It completely ignores everything that our brain had to learn about engaging the right muscles, interpreting haptic feedback via the nervous system, controlling our center of gravity and so much more.

It's rare that an online course will ever take a participant all the way to the level of unconscious competence. This is the level of experience and expertise that takes years of practice and skills refinement to achieve.

It is, however, very likely the level that *you* are operating at. As a course creator, you know so much and are so good at what you do, you don't even realize it. You may even *devalue* how much you know, which leads to what Tanya Geisler calls the Impostor Complex:

> Impostor Complex is that harrowing experience of not being able to fully (and truthfully) internalize your successes.
>
> It's chronic, repetitive ... AND? Overcome-able. Allow it to serve as a reminder that you have strong values of excellence, mastery and integrity.
>
> In other words: actual frauds don't feel like frauds.

If you want to learn more about the Impostor Complex—and how to overcome it—make sure to check out Tanya's work, linked in the references section at *http://beyondsatisfactionbook.com/ bonuses.*

Where Are Your Participants on Their Learning Journey?

Let's now bring this back to the subject of customer satisfaction.

As mentioned, participants in our courses typically come to us in stage two of the competence matrix: they know there is something for them to learn, and that fact has made them uncomfortable enough to want to do something about it.

The challenge in stage two is the incompetence part. While you can create and sell training to address the incompetence, the truth is, it's not an instant fix. And moving out of stage two and into stage three is going to require the participant to make some mistakes—potentially a lot of mistakes.

But how does a participant know they have made mistakes? On their own, they won't. By definition, they are still incompetent. As such, they do not have the experience of knowing what competence actually means.

You might think that this problem goes away in stage three, when a participant becomes aware of their skill level (they are conscious of their competence). And while that can be true to some degree, it's important to remember that even in stage three, they still aren't a master. They're still learning, still making mistakes, still misunderstanding and mis-applying what you're teaching them.

In fact, the problem can be exacerbated by the simple fact that by the time they've reached stage three, participants have gained a great deal of confidence in their own abilities—potentially to the point of overconfidence.

Even *if* you manage to get a participant all the way up to stage four, they *still* are not well posi-tioned to measure just how much they have learned. At the level of unconscious competence, they will actually have moved into *ignorance* about their level of expertise.

Thus, for all these reasons, for as much as your customers may be able to express their *satisfaction* with their progress, that doesn't mean that they are able to accurately describe just how much of an impact your program has had on them.

To help them—and us—determine and commu-nicate that overall impact, we need to avoid the Satisfaction Trap and instead turn our attention to a measure that goes beyond satisfaction: results.

Your Turn!

The Simplest Way to Get Participants Taking Action

Your Turn! sections appear throughout this book as a way for you to put into practice what you have just read. Each is accompanied by an additional resource, download or guide, which you can find at http://beyondsatisfactionbook.com/bonuses.

If I could banish two words from your vocabulary, they would be "know" and "understand."

Why?

Let's look at an example. Here's a common phrase that you might see on a sales page: "By the end of this course, you will know which social media platforms to use in your business."

Now, let me ask you this: what does that actually mean? Will they know:

- Which are the three biggest platforms out there right now?

- The #1 platform that you think every business owner should be using?

- How to evaluate any platform that they encounter, to know if it's right for their business?

And more importantly, how could you possibly evaluate whether someone truly knows something or not? It's not like you can reach inside their heads and *see* the knowledge or understanding. That's the problem with using the words "know" and "understand." The words are just too non-specific (and subjective) to be meaningful.

Of course, when you really dig down into it, it's easy to see that when we say things like, "I want them to understand X," we're using the word as a sort of shorthand. What we *really* mean is that we want them to be able to *do* something based on that understanding. Maybe you want them to:

- Recite a fact from memory

- Describe it in their own words

- Apply their understanding to achieve a certain result

Or maybe you mean something entirely different.

Now, precise language is valuable for any number of reasons, but I mention it here because unless you get clear on what exactly you want people to be able to do, you'll never be able to create effective activities for your course.

So here's a three-step method for doing just that. To help, I recommend that you download and complete the fillable Understanding to Action Guide. It's available at *http://beyondsatisfactionbook.com/ bonuses.*

Step One: List Your Topics

Every training product, course or program consists of a number of topics. These topics may be big or small, comprehensive or detailed. You may have many, or you may have just a few.

For example, if you're teaching a course about using social media for business, your topics may include "an overview of social media platforms" and "finding where your customers hang out online."

List the main topics you cover in your course. To keep things manageable, try to limit yourself to 5–10 overarching topics.

Step Two: Pick Your Level of Mastery

In math, there's a big difference between memorizing your times tables and being able to use a formula to solve a problem. And there's a big difference between using formulas that you've been given and coming up with brand-new ones.

That's because there are different levels of mastery that one can achieve. When it comes to mental skills, educators have identified six levels of mastery:

1. **Remember:** You can perform pure memory-recall tasks like giving definitions.

2. **Comprehend:** You not only can define a concept, you have grasped its underlying meaning and can explain it in your own words.

3. **Apply:** You are able to follow a specific model, formula or example and use those tools in different and new situations.

4. **Analyze:** You are able to break a concept into its constituent parts and see how those parts relate to each other and to the whole.

5. **Evaluate:** You can establish and use criteria to make judgments about the concept.

6. **Create:** You can put things together in a new way to form something that hadn't existed before.

Now, for each of the topics you outlined, ask the following question: When you think about your Perfect Participant and what they need to be able to do by the end of the program, what level of mastery is that?

To continue the "social media for business" example from the previous step, you may decide that when it comes to the overview of social media platforms, what your participants *really* need to do is be able to *evaluate* platforms for themselves. Thus, you'd select the "evaluating" level of mastery.

Record the appropriate level of mastery for each topic beside it on the list, or in the table found in the Understanding to Action Guide.

Step Three: Pick Your Activity

Finally, once you know exactly what level of mastery your participants need to achieve for each topic, you can start to create activities for each one.

The process is quite simple. If you want participants to evaluate social media platforms, then the activity you will have them do needs to be nothing more complicated than that! Just give them a framework or a tool for making their evaluation (for example, a checklist or a series of questions to ask, along with a rating scale), and then instruct them to go and *do it.*

If you find yourself struggling to turn the mastery level into an activity, it may be that using a more specific verb would help. In the Understanding to Action Guide, you'll find a number of alternative verbs appropriate to each level of mastery. So long as the verb you choose is at the right level of mastery, your activity will be too.

How Natasha Vorompiova Got Participants Taking Action (Case Study)

Natasha Vorompiova is the founder of SystemsRock, a company that helps business owners develop systems so that they will run more smoothly, more effectively and with less heartache.

But when it came to Systematic Success, the course she'd created to help teach that process, she felt like it was missing the mark. The problem wasn't that it was *bad*, per se. She was attracting her Perfect Participants, providing them with great materials and giving them incredible value.

No, the problem was that Natasha felt as though she was having to pull people through the program. She was spending far more time and energy than she ever imagined trying to get people to do the work, never mind finish the entire program. And all that cajoling, encouragement and support wasn't something she'd planned on when she designed the course.

She was feeling burned out, over-stretched and frustrated.

And so were her participants.

Originally, Systematic Success took clients through developing 12 different systems for their business—from client intake and lead generation to financial management and team building.

It was just too much.

So the first thing Natasha did was to dramatically reduce the scope of her program and focus *just* on the specific areas that her Perfect Participants wanted help with the *most*. That change alone was huge; she cut two-thirds of the topics and was able to create a much more relaxed pace for participants. They no longer needed to rush from system to system, but were instead able to dig into each system and actually *implement* it before moving on to the next one.

But there was still more to be done.

While she had *lots* of content, Natasha needed to find ways to engage people and actually get them doing the work of building their systems. And that meant building in exercises—not busywork worksheets, but actual, practical hands-on systems work—without overwhelming them with content.

So she replaced the bulk of her content with bite-sized mini-lessons intended to get people designing and implementing their systems, not just reading about it. Each mini-lesson was structured similarly: a very brief reading exercise, followed by a more in-depth chance to apply.

Just *how* brief is that reading exercise,
you might ask? Check out this example:

1.5 Client Intake: Your Online Scheduler

Read in 45sec.
Complete the assignments below in 5-30min.

You must have an online scheduler. If you don't want to promir
you to book meetings without endless back and forth. Plus, onl
attempt to book a session with someone in a different time zon

As suggested in the previous note, when picking an online sched
and nice-to-have features. These lists will help you when asses:

Look at this article for more ideas [http://systemsrock.com/los

Your Turn:

If you haven't yet decided on an online scheduler, create you
resources in the article I recommended.

Feel free to share your thought process or run your final cho
(https://plus.google.com/u/0/communities/10315966877060:

Add other tasks, a-has, or ideas to *your* My Tasks and A-Ha:

Next: 1.6 Client Intake: Collecting Preliminary Information

Yes, you read that right. This lesson has
less than one minute of reading.

The vast majority of the participants'
time is spent *doing the work* and *getting
results*, rather than mindlessly consuming
content. The program compels them to do
so through its heavy emphasis on action
taking.

Whereas in the previous iteration Natasha reported that people started dropping off or falling behind by the first group coaching call, this time was different. Action was being taken. Homework was being submitted. And all without her having to exhort, cajole and remind.

The structure of the redesigned program ended up doing all of that for her.

By giving step-by-step action steps that required only a minimal amount of content consumption, Natasha was able to keep her clients focused on what matters—doing the work—rather than distracting them with what doesn't.

Part III

Evaluating and Iterating

7

A Better Way to Measure
Success

Your participants may not be able to articulate exactly how much they have learned from you, but there is one thing they can express: the outcomes and visible results of what that learning has done for them.

After all, when a participant raves about your course to a friend, what do they naturally emphasize?

The results and impact of your course on their everyday life.

Consider, too, the importance of results when it comes to garnering compelling testimonials, case studies and success stories. Marketers and copywriters know that your sales messages will be far more compelling when you can tell stories that emphasize results, rather than generic references from another "happy customer."

Results are, in aggregate, a far more valuable metric for success than satisfaction could ever be.

This isn't just true in business, though.

Educators, too, recognize the primacy of results when it comes to evaluating training. That's why, to help measure the quality and effectiveness of a training program, they use a four-level evaluation method first developed by Donald Kirkpatrick in 1954.

And as you'll soon see, this method not only addresses the quality of the learning experience itself, but also how that quality can be a significant driver of your business's impact.

Level One: What's Their Reaction?

Just like we instinctively start looking at a product's effectiveness by measuring customer satisfaction, Donald Kirkpatrick argued that we should start by evaluating the participants' reaction to the training: how well did they like the learning process?

But as discussed previously, liking something doesn't mean much. In fact, research now shows that a student's reaction to training is actually a really poor indicator of the training's *effectiveness*.

What does work, though, is looking at how *motivated* people are to complete the training. As it turns out, motivation is not only an incredible indicator of success (motivated students learn more), but it also directly relates to satisfaction and engagement levels (motivated students keep coming back for more).

Ultimately, it's very, very difficult to do something that will change an individual's motivation level—even our own! That's why BJ Fogg, a Stanford researcher who specializes in behavioral psychology, teaches that the key isn't to try to *change* motivation levels, but instead to help people ride their natural waves of motivation.

According to Fogg, it's not motivation itself that makes the difference; it's whether your motivation level matches the challenge being presented. When you are highly motivated, you can do hard things. When you're not highly motivated, even doing simple things can be a challenge.

That's why it's so important to keep your course materials and exercises incredibly doable. The more you can break things down and keep people focused on step-by-step micro-actions, the more likely it is that they will find success and *want* to continue.

For example, most course participants are highly motivated when they first purchase a course. That high motivation is the perfect time to assign a task that's simple to do, but potentially challenging to complete.

Since one of the biggest challenges many participants have in completing courses is making the time to do so, getting them to commit to a certain amount of time—and block it off in their calendar—is a perfect way to harness that motivation.

It might also be worthwhile to proactively ask your participants to plan for things that could potentially prevent them from following through on their goals; for an example of how we've used this technique in our training programs, check out the case study at the end of this chapter.

Finally, as time goes on, you'll want to monitor motivation levels and make sure that what you're asking of people doesn't surpass their ability *or motivation* to do it. The more times you offer your course, the more you'll be able to observe patterns for when motivation is flagging. At a certain point, for example, you may notice participants start logging in less, opening fewer emails, participating in fewer discussions and so on.

In Chapter 9, we'll discuss ways to collect and evaluate feedback from your participants to discern exactly why this is happening, but for now, just recognize that these are warning signs that your participants' motivation levels may not be as strong as they should be.

Level Two: Are They Learning?

Motivation is, of course, just the beginning. You can have the most motivated student in the world, but unless you are effective in helping them on their learning journey, they're going to struggle to get out of the gate.

That's why the second level in Kirkpatrick's method is to see if your course actually results in learning. It's the answer to questions like, "Did my participants learn what they were supposed to?" and more importantly, "Can they do the things they should be able to?"

In traditional education, this is where tests and homework come in. But tests in particular have their own problems (test anxiety, anyone?). Fortunately, there are better ways to see if your participants have actually learned anything.

For example, you can offer critiques and feedback, either as a core part of your offer or as a value-added up-sell. While not everyone will be interested in getting peer or instructor feedback, your Active Participants will see it as a major draw. You'll be able to charge a premium and evaluate how much they've learned, all in one fell swoop.

Another method might be to pay special attention to the discussions happening in your Facebook group, in comments or on live calls, and actively comb those for insights. Track the questions people ask, and you'll quickly be able to see where people are struggling and where they're thriving.

Finally, there's no substitute for embedding activities and self-assessments into the framework of the course itself. As noted in Chapter 5, reflective activities are incredibly valuable; not only do they help solidify learning, but they also help you and your participants recognize the transformation that's happening.

Consider asking them things like: "What's the biggest a-ha moment you had this week/module?" "How has your perception of ____ changed?" or "What did you notice this week when you ____?"

By giving people the opportunity to self-assess and reflect, you're getting them to acknowledge (to you and to themselves) how much they've learned.

Plus, if you are using a membership site or learning management system to deliver your curriculum, you can use a form or survey tool to embed the reflective prompts right into the learning environment, so you can observe patterns in the results—and hopefully gather some great testimonials, too.

Level Three: Has Their Behavior Changed?

When the rubber hits the road, just knowing facts isn't worth a whole lot. In fact, if you can't translate what you've learned into the real world, many educators would argue you haven't really learned anything at all.

That's why Kirkpatrick's third level looks at whether the participant was able to transfer their newly acquired skills to everyday life—in the workplace, their relationships or whatever the appropriate context is.

That said, it can be trickier to evaluate real-world performance in an online course, since in many ways you're reliant on getting honest responses to follow-up questions.

Much like in level two, your discussion groups can be a gold mine here. If you see someone mention a success or struggle, jump on it! Get specific details as to how they applied what they learned or where they struggled. Siphon through the raw data to get at the real facts underneath.

Obviously, you can also ask your participants whether their learning has had an impact on their behavior in the real world using surveys and the like. Again, though, you have to be careful to look beyond what people say, to what they can actually do.

Being really intentional about when and how you ask for behavior-change information can help with this. For example, every repeat or up-sell customer can be asked what changes they made as a result of previous purchases. Every referral can be asked, "What change did the referrer tell you they experienced that convinced you to buy?" And, as much as possible, every person that exits the course—whether they request a refund or just stop working through the materials—should be asked why.

Most importantly, the best indicator of a course that's successful at facilitating behavior change is one that gets lots of referrals and prompts repeat buyers. When people experience a change, they tell others. When their lives are changed and they can see for themselves that the investment was worth it, they'll be more likely to buy from you again. Simply put, performance drives revenues.

Level Four: Are They Getting the Desired Results?

Finally, the last level of Kirkpatrick's method is simple: it all comes down to results.

Whereas looking at performance answers the question of whether participants were able to transfer the skills to the real world, results tell us whether they are better off for having taken the course. Not only were they motivated, not only did they learn, not only were they able to apply the lessons in a different context, but did it *work.*

This is the step that ties everything back together: your marketing messaging, your sales pitch, your curriculum, your pricing. Everything relates to whether your participant got the promised results and experienced the promised transformation.

The techniques for evaluating results in a distributed online course are similar to evaluating performance, but taken one step further. You can do intake and exit surveys and mine your discussion forums, but here's one more technique you can use that's incredibly powerful:

Make performance check-ins part of the learning experience.

This is especially useful when you pair it with the type of reflective practice that we talked about in Chapter 5. You can create a journal, provide a progress tracking worksheet or even just have regular discussion prompts that ask participants to discuss the real-world changes they've experienced.

And, of course, don't forget the follow-up.

Depending on the nature of your program, think about how long it will take before someone can really start seeing measurable results. In some cases, that will happen right away. In others, it might take a while.

Whatever the right timeframe is, remember to follow-up with your participants after the program is complete and ask them what's happened since they finished.

The important thing here is to focus on measurable results. A five-star rating is nothing compared to a testimonial that says "I tripled my business," "I gained five hours a week to spend with my kids," "I no longer go to the cupboard for junk food three times a day" or "It only took me a week before I was playing Billy Joel's 'The Piano Man.'"

The moment you can put numbers behind your sales and marketing, your revenues will skyrocket. Great courses do that for you.

The Bonus Level

In the decades since Kirkpatrick originally proposed this four-level evaluation method, his work has been built upon and expanded by many other educational professionals.

The most common adaptation adds a fifth level to the model, representing return on investment (ROI). For the business owner who intends to sell their courses and demonstrate that the value of the course is far greater than the investment required, ROI is a critical measure.

Simply put, if customers don't feel as though they've received enough value for their money, they'll never refer you to others, nor will they be inclined to become repeat buyers.

ROI is also useful for helping you set your prices. Personally, I like to set pricing such that my clients can expect to see a $5\times$ to $10\times$ return within two years.

That's why it was such a shock when, the first time I ran a group program, one of my participants reported seeing a nearly $100\times$ ROI *in the first year alone.* But it also gave me the confidence to significantly increase my rates, so that they now more accurately reflect the value I bring to the table.

But what do you do if the promised outcome of your course or business isn't directly tied to money? One great strategy is to look at the money that your participants might otherwise have spent in trying to solve their problem.

Say, for example, your business specializes in helping people—especially middle-aged professional women—de-stress so they can sleep better at night. What else might they spend money on in an attempt to solve that problem? Perhaps weekly massages, regular manicures and girls' nights to treat themselves, a new high-end mattress or a battery of medical tests. And those are just the financial costs; it doesn't even consider the mental, physical and emotional costs that stress and lack of sleep can bring.

So consider: *What **is** that return for **your** customers?*

If you're not sure, go back to your Perfect Participant notes from the first Your Turn! section. Since value *is* in the eye of the beholder, it's ultimately your participants who determine what the return is that they seek. If you need more guidance, check out the 5 Questions to Ask resource found at *http://beyondsatisfactionbook.com/bonuses.*

When you can show how your work has helped others see a dramatic return on their investment, it also helps both existing and future customers recognize the value of what you're selling.

By framing your product's value in terms of ROI, you're able to create even more effective messaging and compelling pricing. This not only helps prospects (and repeat buyers) be more willing to invest their hard-earned cash with you, but they'll also be more likely to take it seriously when they do.

And when *that* happens, they see bigger trans-formations, and you have a bigger impact.

Win-win.

Inside The Master Class (Case Study)

For the past several years, I've been offering a group program of my own. It's called The Master Class, and it's designed and intended to help online business owners create trans-formational learning experiences—the types of experiences we've been talking about in this book.

Since it was first developed, the pro-gram has gone through a lot of updates and changes, both to make the program stronger and more effective, and also in response to changes in the market. And at each step along the way, I've been using Kirkpatrick's levels to guide my decisions about what to change and what not to.

Making improvements at the first level, that of the participants' reaction and motivation, was one of the first areas I focused on.

The first few times I tested the program, I found that there was one module in particular that participants struggled with. It came midway through the program, the point at which their motivation levels had naturally started to wane, and they were less inclined to do the intensive, challenging work required.

Very early on, then, I realized I needed to restructure the course. The early modules, which participants typically flew through with ease, were shortened and compressed. That meant that they could get to the challenging portions sooner, when their motivation levels were still high. After further testing, I also decided to split the offending section of the course into two, and later three, parts. Now, participants still report that the program *challenges* them, but it no longer stops them in their tracks.

At the second of Kirkpatrick's levels, for the most part, the program was successful from the outset. For example, as I observed my participants talking about their courses with others on social media, I noticed they were starting to use some of the vocabulary found in The Master Class—a good sign that they were learning something!

It wasn't all perfect, though. Occasionally, I would notice that the concepts the participants were applying weren't being used quite correctly. Other times, it became apparent that participants had a hard time seeing how to apply what they were learning to their own case. To overcome this challenge, we integrated hot-seat coaching, which had the benefit of not only providing additional examples to participants, but encouraging them to share their work and reflect on it alongside us.

One place that The Master Class has always been successful is in helping people apply what they are learning outside of the course itself. Many participants have shared that taking The Master Class has not just affected how they develop courses; they also find that focusing on results and transformation makes things like writing sales and marketing copy easier, too. This is an example of Kirkpatrick's third level: taking skills and behaviors learned in one context and applying it in another.

The fourth level, of course, is results. When I first developed The Master Class, the results were strong, but slow in coming. Participants would plan out their course but not sell it for another six or twelve months—no bueno. However, I knew that actually making money from their course was the ultimate result that my participants were after, so I introduced new material about sales earlier in the program to get them selling faster.

This approach was so successful that one of our participants, Mindy Crary, reported, "Before we had even finished The Master Class, I had $5,000 in my pocket and a 23% conversion rate on my pilot offer."

Finally, the bonus level—ROI. As I mentioned in the previous chapter, the first time

I offered The Master Class, the results were so far beyond my expectations that I ended up having one client make $100\times$ her investment back within a matter of months.

As we continued to refine the program, the ROI remained strong, which ultimately contributed to a significant partnership with Tara Gentile. The Master Class is now licensed to her company and the program is offered exclusively as part of her product line—something which would never have been possible if we hadn't spent the time and energy to get the highest level of results and the biggest success for our students.

8

Gathering Data and the GIGO Problem

Over the past few chapters, we've talked a lot about what it takes to craft a learning experience that keeps participants engaged.

Some of you may be thinking, *This all sounds good, but it really doesn't seem like rocket science.* That's true; it's not.

But too many course producers have the perception that all you need to have in order to make buckets of money is to toss together a course and put it out there. Or they're so afraid to ask for feedback that they put it off for a day that never comes.

Regardless of the reason for burying your head in the sand, the result is always the same: courses and products that create high drop-out or refund rates, no referrals, terrible word of mouth, mediocre reviews, no testimonials and a disincentive to ever buy from that content producer again.

Fortunately, you now have the foundation to avoid becoming one of them. To stand out amongst an unending onslaught of terrible courses, you can't settle for mediocrity. In fact, you must actively work to rise above it.

The success of your participants, your course and your business is too important to leave to chance. To ensure it, you can't just rely on anecdotal evidence or your gut instincts. If you want to create something truly remarkable, you're going to need to start collecting some data.

What to Look For (Especially for the Data-Intimidated)

Now, some people hear the word "data" or "metrics" and immediately start to panic. If that's your instinct, I want to encourage you: this doesn't have to be complicated, but you do need a system to provide you with the data.

You may also be afraid of what the data will say, but the truth is that not asking doesn't change peoples' perception of your course. Collecting data, and then adjusting based on what it tells you, can.

Ultimately, the simplest systems for collecting and analyzing data are *human* systems, based on observation, pattern finding and problem solving.

For example, if you get a request for a refund or notice someone's participation in your course dropping, here's some data you probably already have at your fingertips:

- What reasons did they give for requesting the refund? *(If you don't ask, you won't know)*

- How much time passed since their initial purchase? *(Your payment processor should have this information)*

- What was the last successfully completed section of the course, and how long ago did they complete it? *(If you ask for homework to be submitted, you'll have a record of this)*

- How did the student initially find out about the program? What was their referring source? *(I ask this when people register for a course, so that I have this information available)*

Even with just this information, you have a lot to work with. It tells you when and where motivation has waned, where they were struggling to learn and what they weren't satisfied with. And—if you really dig in—you can even start to intuit what results your participants expected that weren't delivered.

With this information in hand, you can start to make decisions.

Do you need to rework sections of your curriculum? Maybe break up a complex topic into smaller pieces? Perhaps you need to do a better job of setting expectations, or incorporate more hands-on learning opportunities.

The important thing to remember is that it's only when you start *asking these questions* that you can determine what changes need to be made to improve your retention—as well as your referrals and repeat buyers.

Of course, it's never a good idea to make decisions based on just one person's experience. There are a multitude of reasons that an individual may be less engaged. Real life may have interfered, or they may not have been right for your program in the first place (which may indicate a problem with your marketing, not the product itself!).

Data Doesn't Tell a Complete Story

The real key, though, is to not just look at the data itself, but to actively interpret it. You need to put on your detective hat and start looking for patterns and similarities, so that you can make the right decisions going forward.

Here's a fun example that very clearly shows why. Recently, a client was raving to me about how much she loved her new FitBit. "There's only one problem," she said. "I have to remember to take it off when I'm on a coaching call!"

See, in the hour and a half she had spent sitting at her computer talking to clients the day before, her FitBit registered some 4,000 steps. Apparently, she's a hand-talker.

Now, lest you think this is a one-off problem, a similar thing happened when I was on a trail ride with some friends. After a couple of hours of riding, they all dismounted and checked their phones and were delighted to discover that they'd received quite a few badges and awards for the number of flights of stairs they had climbed.

Never mind that their horses had done all the *actual* climbing.

The problem, of course, is that wearable tech is just tech.

As such, it is subject to the same problem that I became oh-so-familiar with as a computer science student, and which also plagues a lot of training businesses today.

The GIGO Problem

Computers are perfectly logical devices, much to the chagrin of developers the world 'round. Digital devices don't care about what you *meant* when you wrote that line of code, nor what behavior you *intended* for them to take.

No, they're simple machines: they do exactly what they are told.

If you ask a computer to do some ridiculous arithmetic—say, add a cat to a dog, then divide by 5—under normal circumstances, it'll spit out an equally ridiculous answer.

Thus, GIGO: Garbage In, Garbage Out.

We humans aren't so perfect in our applications of logic; in fact, our ability to apply logic is downright sad. And yet, at a basic level, we still suffer the same underlying problem as a computer: when we get garbage data in, we often come to some pretty ridiculous conclusions.

That's why it's so important to make sure we're collecting and focusing on the *right* data.

Collecting Data across Four Diagnostic Categories

There are lots of metrics you can use to benchmark your course's success and then iterate and experiment to make improvements. You can probably interpolate many of them from the concepts outlined in previous chapters.

Which are the right ones, though?

In general, I like to focus on metrics that fit into the following four diagnostic categories:

- Retention, Refund and Growth Rates

- Participant-Content Interaction

- Interpersonal Engagement

- Customer Success and Results

Within each category, there are many different aspects you can choose to track and examine; I've included a few examples below, and you can find a full list of potential success metrics among the resources at *http://beyondsatisfactionbook.com/bonuses.*

Retention, Refund and Growth Rates

At a basic level, this first category of metrics is quite simple. You probably have an intuitive sense of the numbers, even if you're not actively tracking them.

It's important not to ignore data, though, in favor of just relying on our intuition, if for no other reason than confirmation bias: you'll pay more attention to anecdotes that support your pre-existing beliefs and less to anything that doesn't fit your existing narrative.

If you believe your program is good, for example, you're likely to overestimate your retention rates. On the other hand, if you have doubts about the quality of your work, you'll be more prone to overreact to even a single refund.

With that being said, here are some ideas for where to begin:

- How many participants who were active at the start of the reporting period were still active at the end?

- What percentage of participants ask for their money back (usually within a defined period such as 30 or 60 days of purchase)?

- How far into the program do participants get before dropping out or requesting a refund?

Finally, if you run a membership community or evergreen course with rolling enrollments, consider also tracking your *growth rate:* the number of participants in the course at the end of the reporting period compared to the start.

Growth rate is the metric that tells you whether you are gaining more paying customers than you are losing at any given time. A simple way to think about and track your growth rate is to frame it in terms of monthly recurring revenue (MRR). If your MRR is increasing month over month, you have a positive growth rate. If not, then you don't.

Participant-Content Interaction

Remember, a participant's interaction with the content of your course has been identified by researchers as a strong predictor of student satisfaction. And of course, participants actually working through your course content also correlates positively with stronger student results.

The questions you should be seeking answers to in this category all focus around measures related to completion. For example, consider ways you might be able to discern:

- What percentage of participants successfully access the course materials *(log in to site, open/click through in an email, etc.)*?

- For each section *(module, lesson, etc.)* of the course, how long does it take participants to start and complete any activities *(assessments, exercises, worksheets, discussion, etc.)*?

- How often does the average participant view/review course materials, and which materials are viewed/reviewed most often?

As you consider these questions, though, be careful not to fall into the trap of over-emphasizing completion. Remember, it is possible for your participants to achieve transformation without completing. Your Passive Participants can still end up achieving phenomenal results and being amazing advocates for your course. It's just that when they do complete, they will be able to benefit that much *more*.

Interpersonal Engagement

The second best predictor of student satisfaction, as you may recall, is their perception that an instructor is available to answer their questions and provide support.

This can be hard to measure; after all, many course creators intentionally try to minimize the amount of time and energy they (and their teams) have to spend engaging with participants. When it comes to evaluating on the basis of interpersonal engagement, then, it's useful to focus on what channels you *do* have available for support.

- Do you have a customer service team? If so, how many questions do they get, and how many participants are using that resource?

- What about your discussion groups? How many new threads are posted each week, and by how many different people?

- If you offer coaching calls, what is attendance like? How many people attend week after week, and how many just pop in now and again?

Again, it's not so much that you need to offer all these types of support; rather, look at what forms of support you *are* offering and then consider how many participants are aware of those supports—and how many actively use them.

Customer Success and Results

Finally, we come to the diagnostic category that will have the biggest impact on your business: customer success and results.

The most obvious way to evaluate customer success is simply to follow up with them after the course is complete, asking them what results they saw.

But remember, it's always more important to focus on what people *do* rather than simply accepting what they *say* at face value. That's why I recommend looking for other indicators that customers have been successful, notably:

- What percentage of customers actively recommend your product?

- What is the lifetime value of each of your customers?

- How much revenue does the product generate in terms of cross-sells and up-sells?

If these questions sound familiar, they should: as we've seen over and over throughout this book, the ultimate measure of customer success and results is their willingness to refer others and become repeat buyers themselves.

That said, if you find yourself struggling to get the kinds of referrals and testimonials you believe your course is worthy of, consider whether you're doing everything you can to garner them. In the resources provided at *http://beyondsatisfactionbook. com/bonuses*, we've included a copy of our Remarkable Referrals guide to help.

Choose the *Right* Metrics

As you can see, there is no shortage of quantitative data you can collect when it comes to evaluating your course and diagnosing potential problem points.

What's important to realize is that you don't have to track everything; it's more important to choose 2–3 metrics that you can directly tie to profit and revenue. For example, you may choose to focus on overall completion rates and the number of quality testimonials.

Whatever you choose, remember to focus on things that you can actually *have an impact on*, and which will *make the biggest impact* on your business's success. In the case study that follows this chapter, I'll show you how one business owner did just that, with dramatic results.

But quantitative data isn't the only data that we have at our fingertips. If you found yourself reading through this section and wondering, *What about the feedback **my** participants provide?* never fear: that's where we're headed next.

How Cory Huff Solved His Retention Problems, Got More Testimonials and Increased Sales (Case Study)

Cory Huff is the founder of The Abundant Artist, a training and coaching company dedicated to helping artists sell their art online.

When Cory came to us, his flagship course had hit a revenue ceiling. No matter what he and his team tried, sales weren't increasing. Plus, while one-on-one clients saw amazing results, Cory hadn't been able to fully translate that same success into the course.

Fortunately, the data revealed two core problems that, once addressed, led to his most successful cohort ever.

The first problem, according to Cory, was retention. In his words, "Nobody sticks around and stays engaged." When we looked closer at the data, we found that only 5% of participants wound up completing the course. In fact, when we examined participant behavior, we found that virtually no one was watching the hour-long videos. It didn't fit into their life, their schedule or their plans, so they didn't do it.

Even among participants who did complete the course, though, Cory found it incredibly difficult to get quality testimonials. This was the second problem: he wasn't able to get the types of referrals, case studies or success stories that would help sell his course again in the future.

Fortunately, solving both these issues came down to two simple steps.

First, we recommended that each week's material be broken down: chop the videos from hour-long modules to laser-focused 10-to-15-minute lessons, and deliver them in smaller batches throughout the week.

Second, we advised Cory that if each video was accompanied by a specific task (worksheet, homework assignment, etc.), that would get participants taking action immediately.

Whereas previously the course was 90% content, the newly revised version was designed to get participants spending 60% of their time applying what they were learning.

The results were dramatic.

When Cory next offered this same course, the retention rate for the course skyrocketed to more than 6X the previous rate.

Not only were participants retained more effectively, but their results improved dramatically. In fact, by embedding action steps throughout the course materials, nearly half of the participants saw results while the course was in session.

In the past, Cory had gotten just a handful of mediocre testimonials, but now that students were making dramatic transformations across the board, they were all too happy to share their victories. As a result, the testimonials and success stories for the course improved dramatically, in both number and quality.

The next time Cory launched his course, his sales had improved 30%, demolishing his previous best sales numbers and paving the way for rapid future expansion and growth.

9

Making the Most of Customer Feedback

There is no better example of the GIGO problem than when it comes to collecting and interpreting customer feedback.

Take this scenario: You've just finished delivering your program for the first time, and you want to know what suggestions your participants have for improving it in the future. So, you ask them for feedback.

"I loved it!" one person says, while another says, "I wasn't impressed."

"I was overwhelmed!" says one person. "I felt like it didn't go deep enough!" responds another.

This scenario would be funny if it weren't so common.

But contradictions in customer feedback *are* common, and they are a clear marker that feedback is imperfect. There is, to use the language of GIGO, a lot of garbage cluttering up the value and obscuring the truth.

The Inherent Flaws of Feedback Formulas

As we saw earlier, the biggest problem, of course, is that your customers aren't experts. That is, quite literally, why they come to you for training.

They don't know what they don't know, so any feedback they give you is bound to be imperfect. And yet, you're told over and over how important it is to collect feedback so you can iterate and improve.

Where you end up is smack dab in the middle of a catch-22: the place where feedback is both incredibly valuable... and completely useless.

This isn't what most people will tell you, of course.

No, they'll give you formulas to follow. Survey questions to ask. Processes for analysis. Methods for figuring out which responses to pay attention to and which to ignore.

But all of those formulas suffer the same fatal flaw as computers do: garbage in, garbage out.

Even if you object to the notion that feedback could be garbage, you have to admit that at best, feedback is notoriously *messy* data. There will undoubtedly be some gems, but it's going to take a more sophisticated approach if we're to find them.

Start by Asking Better Questions

The first problem that we run into when it comes to seeking feedback is with the very questions we ask.

Take, for example, the typical question we ask in our pursuit of feedback: "What do you think?"

This is, quite simply, a meaningless question, one of the most meaningless you can ask. What do they think about *what?*

No matter how you dress it up, or what fancy words you use, when you ask people for generic feedback like this, it's too broad and too open to interpretation.

We need to be *more clear* on what exactly we're asking our customers for, and we must realize that when we ask blanket questions under the guise of seeking "feedback," we're doing more harm than good.

Instead, you need to do more of the work upfront and learn to ask better questions of your participants.

When someone asks, "What did you think?" for example, they *usually* mean something like:

- "What results did you get?"

- "Where did you struggle?"

- "What expectations did you have that were (or weren't) met?"

If this is the type of information you seek, then what you should be doing is asking *those* questions. Don't expect your customers to read your mind; after all, you're the expert, not them!

Questions Aren't Good Enough

Even more than just asking better questions, though, you can find even richer feedback in other ways. It's not found in what they *say*. Instead, it's to be found in their actions. Consider:

- What questions do they ask? This reveals places where your explanations were not clear, or where you jumped from A to D without addressing B or C.

- What exercises do they fail to complete? This reveals exercises that feel too challenging for their current levels of motivation. You need to either provide better support resources or make the activity simpler.

- What tasks do they accomplish, but poorly? This reveals a skill they have not yet mastered, a place where you may need to provide more support and guidance about how to do it well and how to self-assess one's progress.

When you look at their *behavior*, you'll find far more valuable feedback and information about what's working—and what's not working—in your program.

Here's another way of thinking about it: we know that people learn by doing. That's been amply demonstrated throughout this book, has been proven time and time again by the research community and also rings true when we consider our own personal experience as students.

As such, it is *in our participants' ability to **do** the things they need to **do*** that we can judge where our programs and courses are successful and where they fail.

My favorite description of learning exemplifies this: we know learning has occurred when the student has the opportunity to *choose differently* than they might have chosen before.

Note the verb in the sentence: "choosing" is an action, a behavior. Thus, our participants' behavior is the only *real* measure of whether our program has been successful—whether it has helped them to achieve the transformation that they sought for themselves, and the transformation that we intended for them to undergo.

The Hallmarks of Changed Behavior

Which exact behavioral cues you're looking for, of course, depends on the nature of the training you're providing. That's where your role as the expert comes in: you should *know* what behaviors demonstrate that a participant has learned what they need to do.

What those things are, exactly, is up to you to define. Your job, as the curriculum creator, is to determine what actions your participants need to take that, when taken together, will create the desired transformation.

In teaching and learning jargon, these are known as learning outcomes: the observable, measurable things that someone must *do* if they are to accomplish their goals. Maybe they'll be able to prepare meals that are nutritionally balanced. Write a sales page that converts. Touch their toes with a flat back. Demonstrate compassion in a tough situation.

Whatever those actions are, it's essential that you clearly define them so you can then measure your participants' progress against their ability to complete them.

Managing the Perception Gap

As a business owner, you must also come to terms with the fact that sometimes, our participants have different ideas than we do about what success looks like.

Sometimes, we're thrilled with their progress, but they feel as though they should be further along. Or conversely, they feel like they've conquered the world, and we can only see how amateur their efforts really are.

The first thing to acknowledge is that this perception gap is completely normal—and in many ways should be expected. Again, your participants are not experts, so their views on what is possible are colored by their lack of expertise.

That doesn't mean, however, that you can ignore your participants' definitions of success. After all, value *is* in the eye of the beholder, and your participants are the ultimate arbiters of whether they have received value from your course.

But how do you determine if they feel like a success?

Well, you could simply ask them the question, but that takes us back to the realm of messy data and feedback.

No, instead we must again turn our attention to behavioral cues. In this case, we need look no further than the three Rs we established at the outset:

Are they referring your program to their friends and colleagues? Are they retained through to the end of the course? Are the same customers making repeat purchases, buying from you again and again?

As we've seen time and time again, those actions reveal far more about the effectiveness of your program than simply asking for feedback ever could.

The Key to Continuous Improvement

Now, that's not to say that a course that gets regular referrals, no refunds and a slew of repeat buyers is perfect.

There's always room for improvement.

Every time I—or one of my clients—run a program, we always do a post-program assessment.

We gather data from all kinds of sources; we look at the three Rs first and foremost. That gives us the most true information, because it's based on customer behavior (which doesn't lie). But we also consider additional data points: Frequently asked questions. Community participation levels. Instructor observations. And—yes—customer feedback.

See, just because feedback is messy doesn't mean it's useless. Rather, it's that feedback must be used as one of many tools.

Ultimately, what you want to do is first use data and behavioral cues to diagnose where your course or program may have problems. Then, you can collect *valuable* feedback by asking specific questions of your participants, questions like:

- "I noticed that you seemed to struggle with the exercise at the end of module one. Can you tell me more about that?"

- "We've seen many questions come up around Topic X. Here's another explanation; does this help to clarify?"

- "What's the biggest challenge you're encountering right now as you try to apply this lesson?"

The answers to these more *specific* questions, taken together with the observational data you've already collected, are worth more than any generic feedback could ever be.

It's by analyzing *all* of this information that you'll be able to continuously improve on your program, achieving better participant results, stronger retention and referrals, an increase in repeat buyers and ultimately, work that has a greater impact on the world.

Your Turn!

Finding Where to Make Course Corrections

Your Turn! sections appear throughout this book as a way for you to put into practice what you have just read. Each is accompanied by an additional resource, download or guide, which you can find at http://beyondsatisfactionbook.com/bonuses.

So if examining participant behavior tells you what needs to change—but not necessarily why— and collecting feedback isn't the answer, what exactly do you do? How do you figure out what to change?

To answer those questions, you must first have a clear vision of what success looks like in your course or program. Otherwise, you have nothing to measure against. So before you start worrying about how to improve your course, you first need to be crystal clear on what exactly it's supposed to do.

If you haven't already completed the previous Your Turn sections, I recommend doing that now. The Perfect Participant exercise will help you clearly articulate what success looks like in your course and the Understanding to Action process will turn that success into observable, measurable actions your Perfect Participants will be able to take when they've completed your program.

Once you've done that, you can start the evaluation process.

Part I: Mid-Program Evaluations

One of the biggest problems we get ourselves into is when we ignore all indications of how things are working (or not) while they're happening.

Big mistake.

Put it this way: how did you feel about the lunch you ate three weeks ago Thursday? Unless that day happened to be the birthday of someone close to you (or maybe yours, in which case, happy belated birthday!), you probably don't have the first clue.

That's what it's like when we wait until the end of a program to collect feedback. At best, you get hazy recollections. At worst, you get information that's just plain wrong. Instead of waiting until the very end of the program, then, it's important to be monitoring participant progress throughout your program.

To do this, start by identifying where in your program your participants will be asked to do (or attempt to do) the key actions that you identified in the previous Your Turn section. Then, pay specific attention during those parts of the program. Watch your participants to see if they are successful at completing those core actions. If they are, then well done! You've given them what they need to succeed. If not, then that's a sign that revision and rework is necessary.

Remember, the most important thing you can do is observe what your participants are doing through the learning process. When they ask you questions, share victories, post progress updates or showcase their new skills, that is *actual, real evidence* that points to where your program is working and where it's not.

So keep track of the questions they ask, the victories they share and so on. Tally up how many times these things come up—and when—and use that information to help you determine what's working and what's not.

Part II: Post-Program Evaluations

The work doesn't end once your program does, of course. In fact, it's at course completion that you have the best opportunity to evaluate the overall effectiveness and impact of your program.

Whereas the mid-program evaluations described above can help you identify individual things to adjust or tweak, it's only by looking at the whole that you can really see how the pieces fit together.

For this, in addition to collecting the data outlined in Chapter 8, I do recommend conducting a survey or interviews.

In particular, you want to ask questions such as:

1. What was the #1 concern or challenge that you had before making the decision to take this course? *(In other words, what was their goal when they registered?)*

2. What is the #1 result you saw as a result of the course? *(In other words, what do **they** believe was the most significant transformation they achieved?)*

3. What are three other benefits you received? *(This question invites them to go beyond the obvious and reflect on deeper transformation.)*

4. Is there anything you would have changed about your experience, or can you recommend any improvements? *(By asking this question **after** asking people about their positive experiences, you predispose them to provide constructive criticisms rather than just negative rants.)*

And of course, if your data or mid-program evaluations revealed any particular challenge spots or potential problems, you will want to ask specific questions to help you discover *why* those issues may have manifested.

Finally, visit *http://beyondsatisfactionbook.com/bonuses*, where we've included a brief video to help you interpret the answers you get to these questions, so you can be confident that you're changing the *right* things.

A Word of Advice: Don't Change Everything at Once

When I was working in higher ed, we frequently would redesign entire diploma programs in one fell swoop. Top to bottom, every course would get an update and a refresh.

Sometimes it worked, but not always.

I remember distinctly a conversation with one of my colleagues about this. She said, "I don't know why we do it this way. Change doesn't always make things better."

She was right.

Sometimes, in trying to fix things that are broken, you can accidentally change things that are working.

The bigger the changes, the more likely it is that you will inadvertently break something that was working.

So as you conduct your evaluations, resist the temptation to make wholesale changes. Instead, focus on iterating and making ongoing tweaks. Making those specific changes will be far less time-consuming for you and far more impactful for your participants.

Where Online Courses Are Headed Next

Crafting learning experiences that have massive impact isn't a one-step process.

It's something you need to work on over time. You need to be willing to iterate, improve and constantly be on the lookout for a new edge. Why?

Because markets are not stagnant.

They are, after all, made up of people—customers—who change and evolve over time.

Nowhere is this more true than in the world of online education.

A few years ago, you could stand out in the market simply by having a course. Today, the landscape has changed. The market is no longer willing to pay attention just because you have a course. Now, you have to do something different.

Unlocking the Secrets of Market Sophistication

Eugene Schwartz, author of the seminal marketing book *Breakthrough Advertising*, relates this change in the market to a phenomenon called market sophistication.

According to Schwartz, when you first bring an innovative product to a new market, that new idea alone is enough to get attention and capture buyers. That's why a few years ago, having a course was enough—because no one else was doing it.

However, your success inevitably catches the eye of competitors. They begin to join the market, and soon it's no longer enough just to have a course. Instead, you have to outdo the competition. This is known as enlarging your claim: you make bigger and better claims about your bigger and better product.

Of course, eventually people start to become dubious of these too-good-to-be-true claims. You can't just say, "My product is better!" Rather, when the market reaches this level of sophistication, you need to show how your product is different, using facts that prove your claims are legitimate.

This is the path that the online training marketplace has taken over the past few years: from courses being unique and unusual, to needing to make bigger and better claims in your marketing, to requiring extensive social proof in the form of testimonials and success stories.

Schwartz's framework did not end with enlarged claims, though, and neither has the evolution of the market for online courses.

After all, just like there's more than one way to skin a cat, there's more than one course that can get results for customers. And there are only so many times that you can prove that your course gets *even better* results before the claim starts to lose its effectiveness.

The problem is, of course, that in the end we don't buy based on logic, but on emotion. That's why Schwartz argues that there comes a point at which no logical appeal will work.

The market knows so much about what you have to offer and your industry that nothing you say—no proof, no claims, no evidence—will work. To thrive at this level, you need to have a brand affinity that emotionally hooks buyers and keeps them at your side. Think Apple devotees, and you have the idea.

Your Market's Sophistication

Clearly, not every market is at the same point of market sophistication when it comes to online training products. In some niches, it's still very much a blue ocean. You can be the first (or one of the first) to do your thing through a training program, and you'll be successful—until others catch up, of course.

But elsewhere, the market is already past that point. In these markets, customers are more experienced, more sophisticated and harder to convince to buy. These are the markets where people are going on self-proclaimed course-buying moratoriums: they are just so done with the whole idea.

Here's a somewhat meta example, the "selling courses about creating courses" niche. A few years ago, it was enough to simply have a course on the subject. The first to market made a lot of money simply by virtue of being there. Then as more players entered the market, the claims started to enlarge (six-figure courses are so yesterday... let's do seven-figure courses!). Then came the bigger-than-life remarkable case studies and testimonials: the "facts" that proved the claims.

Close behind, undoubtedly, are Schwartz's last two levels, and people will be buying based on brand association alone. I'm already seeing it happen. Are you?

What's more important, though, is this: if it's happening in the online training industry, you can bet it will happen in your industry, too, before long.

The Solution? Do Remarkable Work

The solution, of course, is to create ultra-loyal customers that will continue to buy from us simply because they *love* us. Brand advocates who will buy everything we offer, spread the word about what we do to everyone who will listen and see remarkable transformations as a result of working through our programs.

In other words, the key to overcoming market sophistication and growing your business, even when the market is getting saturated, is to focus on the three Rs: retention, referrals and repeat buyers.

The way to do *that* is to seriously answer the question that too many online business owners only give lip service to:

What does success look like to your customers?

It's easy to talk about customer success. It's especially easy, as business owners, to focus on getting great testimonials and results that we can feature on our blogs and sales pages. And, of course, we also want our customers to be successful, for their own sake and for their own benefit.

That's usually where the conversation ends.

It's rare to stop and ask, "What does customer success *actually look like* here?"

But we should.

Whenever you invite others into your sphere of influence—into your audience, your course, your coaching program or your community—your job is *not* simply to help them overcome the struggle that they are aware of right now.

Your job is to have a vision for what their success can look like, even if they can't see it yet. Your customers need *you* to show them how the struggles they are facing right now fit into the bigger picture, how your course is just one step along the journey. That's what it means to do remarkable work.

As we've seen in this guide, that starts when you focus on the right kind of customers: the kind that want to achieve at the highest level and who are willing to put in the time, effort and energy to do so.

These are the customers that will buy in to your vision and believe that what you say is possible—and then be willing to put in the work to get there, be engaged and satisfied along the way and ultimately see dramatic results.

It All Comes Down to Getting People into Action

Taking action is, after all, the biggest difference maker of them all. Remember, it was the participants' engagement with the course materials and their interaction with the instructors that predicted their satisfaction. It was when students took action by experimenting with the simulated brain that their test scores went up.

In many ways, what you're creating is a virtuous cycle. Satisfied participants are more engaged. That engagement builds their satisfaction. 'Round and 'round the cycle goes.

But even more than that, engagement is what leads to success beyond satisfaction.

That's because we learn by doing. In the end, it's participants' willingness to reflect and apply the learning that leads to deep, transformative learning.

Not by reading about something, or thinking about it or watching a video on it.

By doing.

So if we are going to maximize *our* effectiveness and success as teachers, our goal must not be to create loads of awesome content. No, to be effective, we must invest our energy into helping our participants take the actions that lead to results.

That is the underlying message of Kirkpatrick's four levels for evaluating training success: customer reaction matters, but it's not enough on its own. You must also ensure that your course helps participants to learn. And not just in the safe confines of the learning environment, but in the real world, too.

It's only by focusing on success, results *and* satisfaction that you can beat back the attrition and apathy that threaten your ultimate success. And retaining participants is just the beginning; your ultimate goal should be to turn them into revenue engines who grow your business both by referring new customers to you and by coming back as repeat buyers, time and time again.

That's the foundation for growing your impact and your success in business, and it's something I hope you feel better equipped to tackle now that you've read this book.

Remarkable Work Begins Beyond Satisfaction

Sometimes, people ask me: "What's more important? Having a great product or having great marketing?"

I always respond that the key to a successful product isn't found in either option. It's about having a remarkable product, backed by strong marketing. Both-and, not either-or. You *do* still need to build awareness and trust; you still need to market and sell. But you need to back it up with a great product. You need to deliver on the promises that your marketing makes.

When you do that, you create fans for life. They're the ones that will grow your business more than you ever could on your own.

Remarkable work is what makes your customers want to include you in their conversations. To talk about you to their friends and colleagues. To buy your next thing, and the next thing and the next thing after that.

When we talk about word-of-mouth marketing, that's really what we're talking about: that confluence of satisfaction and results that leads to something that customers can't stop talking about.

That's what happens when you go *beyond satisfaction.*

Further Resources

For a complete set of tools and resources to help you implement the concepts from this book, please visit:

http://beyondsatisfactionbook.com/bonuses

You can also read more from Breanne (and connect with her and her team) at:

http://mnibconsulting.com

Acknowledgements

I now understand why many authors say that the acknowledgements is the hardest part of the book to write. And yet, I know I'd be remiss if I didn't say a deep, heartfelt *thank you* to those whose guidance, contributions and support throughout the process were so instrumental.

First and foremost, thanks must go to Jill: my partner in business and life who never ceases to build me up when I need it, keep me humble when I need *that* and provide me with a patient listening ear at all times.

My friend and colleague Tara Gentile: without your support and encouragement, this book would not exist. Thank you for showing me the value and importance of the work I bring to the world—and for helping me to share it.

Writer of the best foreword ever, Jason Van Orden: when I asked you if you'd write the foreword, you said you'd be honored. Truly, the honor is all mine.

My rockstar editor, Amy Scott: when I came to you asking if you'd help me make Beyond Satisfaction worthy of a second edition, I never imagined this would be the outcome. Your guidance and insights, both as an editor and reader, shaped this book in remarkable ways.

The willing case study participants and also those who contributed their thoughts, expertise and experience: Tanya Geisler, Cory Huff, Marie Poulin, Ali Shapiro, Vanessa Van Edwards and Natasha Vorompiova. Thank you for being an such an example to all future readers.

All of the book launch team members who helped spread the word, provide feedback and support throughout the book's launch: I'm terrified I'd forget someone if I tried to list you all by name, so please just know how much your energy, insights and trust inspired me throughout the process.

And finally, thank you. Whether you're a long-time reader of the blog or this is the first time we've "met"—you are the reason I wrote this. Here's to your success, and the success of all your students.

About the Author

As the founder of MNIB Consulting, Breanne Dyck helps online training businesses scale their impact, their team and their revenue.

Her results-driven strategies blend operations management, business model development and learning & product strategy to create transformational learning experiences that customers can't stop talking about.

Breanne regularly consults on flagship products and programs, CreativeLive courses, live events and workshops for thought-leaders and influencers including bestselling authors Chris Guillebeau, Tara Gentile and Natalie Sisson.

When she's not writing, consulting with clients or speaking, you're likely to find Breanne with her nose in a business book, playing designer board games or building Lego.

Printed in Great Britain
by Amazon